DAWN MAREE

What Does A

RED PILL

Have To Do

With Solving

Your Problem?

Problem Solving Made Easy

What Does A Red Pill Have To Do With Solving Your Problem?
Problem Solving Made Easy

Copyright © 2009 by Dawn Maree

Print ISBN: 978-1-09838-650-4
eBook ISBN: 978-1-09838-651-1

Printed in USA by https://wwwBookBaby.com

Dedication

I dedicate this book to my three amazing Sons.

CONTENTS

CHAPTER 1

The Red Pill

So you have a problem and you need help...right? I mean really, you lost your job and you don't have money for rent, and if that isn't enough, you're getting kicked out of your place to live. You're being attacked by trolls on social media. The love of your life just left you. You're fighting with your close family members because...well in a nutshell...they want to run your life. You have bill collectors pounding on your door, and calling you on the phone. And...dammit your problem has put you in a very uncomfortable place...and **IT HURTS TO BE THERE!**

I get it, let's not waste anytime beating around the bush helping you, but first let me explain to you how a one red pill can help you solve your problem. It was 2016, Donald Trump had just been elected president, and my 23 year old middle Son had a raging addiction to meth and heroin. In order to cope with my Son's addiction, and a bad break-up with an ex, I bought property in eastern Washington State and moved to the top of my very own mountain, just so that I could pull myself back together again.

I was living in an off-grid cabin on one lot, and I had also bought the lot below me for my middle Son to live on, in his own off-grid cabin. I was able to live in this remote place on my own because I had a lucrative online business as a Professional Psychic/Medium, and all I needed was cell reception to run it effectively. Fortunately, I got really good cell reception in my new remote home, and I solved my internet problem by getting two portable hot-spots, one for myself and one for my Son. It was the first time in my 47 year life-time that I had ever been without an official TV or the programming that went with it, and with that said, Facebook, Google and YouTube soon became my best friends. I was able to satisfy my middle Son with his cell-phone, movies that bought at WalMart, and with a subscription to Netflix. Boy Howdy did my world ever change the moment that mountain became my home!

All my life I had been trained to do the same things over and over again. Get up, turn on the news, get ready for work, get the kids ready for school, drop the kids off to school, go to work, get off work, pick the kids up from school, clean the house, cook dinner, sit down and watch the news again and a few TV favorite shows, go to bed, and get up to do it all over again...**FOR 47 YEARS OF MY LIFE.** No wonder I felt like I was stuck in the "Groundhogs Day" movie!

The day I moved to the top of my mountain, was the day I unplugged from the "Matrix" of living a life I had been programmed since childbirth to live. However, I still had yet to take a red pill that would change my life and outlook on it forever. For the first time in my life I was living **IN MY LIFE**, not in programming from a TV box that told me what was going on around me, and how to feel and think about it. I was interacting on a personal level with my neighbors. In town I knew the store cashiers, the waitresses, and the bankers all by their first names. If I wanted news about what was going on around me, I went to the local restaurant and quietly listened to everyone around me as I ate my meal.

With that said, I found it a bit jarring and odd that for the first time in my adult Professional Psychic/Medium life, while living alone on the top of my mountain, a president of the United States came to me for help in a dream. This president that came to me was the out-going president, Barrack Obama. After coming to me once for help, I stopped dreaming about him all together. Truth be told though, I brushed it off after a few days of musing over it, and it wasn't long before I dismissed the dream as just another oddity of mountain life... and then that little red pill hit. What made it worse was that having a honed sense of extra-sensory perception...I didn't see it coming! At this point my focus was on staying afloat financially and getting my auto-biography finished. Inside I had a definite a sense of urgency to get my book finished, because my Son's addiction was getting so bad that I could feel his impending death looming around the corner, and I knew somehow that this would be a game changer.

This was when I took that infamous "red pill" zooming around on YouTube all day, in between Psychic/Medium readings, writing my auto-biography, and and caring for my middle Son. There was so much information put in front of me that was way beyond the scope of normal TV programming. I was mind-blown to hear the stories of Satanic Ritualistic Abuse survivors. To see the pictures of "panda eyed" children, and hear their screams from recordings of what happened to them was to trigger my own PTSD off the charts!. This rocked my world and turned it upside down, as I was thrown back into my own memories of childhood abuse. Seeing all of the stories of "Pizza Gate" and the real documentation that backed it up was too much for my already trauma ridden brain. After a week of digging and getting blown away by who in the government and Hollywood were part of the massive web of people abusing and killing of women and children, I had to shut it down, and push it out of my focus. I already had way too much on my plate with trying to keep my Son from the death grip of drug addiction, while now running two online businesses, learning internet and digital marketing, and finish my auto-biography.

It was after I tried to shut all of my knowing down, that President Trump and his wife Melania came to me for help in my dreams, not once, but three times in a row. I did my best to help them both, and at the end of the three dreams, they bid me farewell, and boarded a bus to leave. I remember that Trump had no problem getting on the bus, but I had to help Melania with a bit of her luggage before she could board the bus. Once again, I didn't really read to much into this as I have never been interested in politics at all. From the time I was born in 1970 with extra-sensory perception, I knew that people in the USA only had the appearance of being free, and I also knew that most of our elections were rigged to serve a 1% elite population.

After doing my best to clear my mind of the musings over the dreams I had about President Trump, his wife, and all the political downloads that kept pulling on my ability to focus, once again, I went back to doing my best to just stay focused on maintaining my two online businesses, writing my auto-biography, and doing everything in my power to not let drug addiction kill my Son. Regardless, Trump seemed to still be a part of my life now simply because so many clients were asking about him in my psychic business. Clients were also very afraid of what the TV media was telling them about Trump being a rich, fat cat, criminal liar that was in bed with the Russians, and because of this, they were asking me a lot of what the future held. My Guide Ephraim kept showing me that things weren't going to be as bad as the TV media was portraying it to be, simply because Trump wasn't really the "bad guy." I was also shown over a period of time that it was actually very dark Deep State people that owned and ran the media, our government, legal system, school system, and health system, that were really the ones that were out to destroy the people in America. Boy howdy do I ever remember the year of 2017 when my Guide kept telling people to stock up on food, toiletries and cleaning goods. It was a bit amusing to say the least, but when all my clients came back to tell me in the spring of 2020 how on target I had been in my predictions, even I couldn't believe what was happening.

As much as I tried to push Trump and the good people that surrounded him out of my mind and my energy field so that I could focus on things in my life, the information about what he was doing to, "drain the swamp," in our government kept seeping in. My neighbor at the base of the mountain kept coming up to give me more and more news on the Trump person he voted into office. My middle Son and his close friend valiantly bragged about the change they had helped to bring to America, in a man that I found had a strange orange color to his skin, but whose eyes emitted a deep energy of strength and compassion.

With this came more information around "Deep Underground Military Bases," and how earthquakes that were 3, 6, and 10 miles deep were caused by our military and a team of good guys rescuing abused women and children from them, and then blowing them up. I couldn't ignore this information either as there were two earthquakes, caused by "D.U.M.B's" being blown up, right underneath my mountain. These earthquakes shook my cabin and everything in it, coming in at 3.4 on the Richter scale for both of them, and they were only two months apart! Yet still in all of this I buried my head in learning internet and digital marketing "fire hose" style from my business mentor, running two online businesses, and doing everything I could to finish my auto-biography.

And then my middle Son died...

...May 22, 2018 @ 9:53am...

...and just like that, my soul was slammed opened to release all the grief that I felt in his change, going off the earth plain. Right behind that was all the grief that was under it from deeply hidden childhood abuse issues.

This was when I shut down completely. Now I truly stopped focusing on anything that had to do with what was going on in the government and/or larger collective, and just focused on my very real problems of grief from my Son dying, my closest family members rejecting me, and huge looming financial problems. When I wasn't crying I was focused on learning marketing, giving Psychic/Medium readings, and finding a way to publish my auto-biography two months after my Son's death. It took me until November of 2019 to recover to a place where I could function enough to help my other two children, and that is exactly what I launched into doing.

As I left my mountain at the beginning of November 2019 on a mission to help my youngest Son in Portland, I realized that I had become a different person. You see I no longer was allowing TV programming to dictate to me what was going on in my world, what I was feeling, or how I should believe. I was now free of fear-based emotions for most of my awake time, and now I was not only free thinking, I was also on a search for truth in every part of my world and life. Oh and what a better place to learn it than from the headquarters of the AntiFa movement itself, Portland Oregon!

Four months after I arrived in Portland, my oldest Son came to live with my youngest Son and I in our High-Rise downtown apartment, and two weeks later the height of the Covid Pandemic hit. After hunkering down for three months in our cozy apartment, the George Floyd riots began, and with it came endless nights of listening to helicopters and tear gas flash-bangs go off all night long. It was then that "Cancel-Culture" and cyber bullying kicked into over-drive, and I could no longer ignore what was going on in politics or government from then on. From eleven stories up in downtown Portland, I was watching our country, we call America, goes straight to hell in a hand-basket. In what was once a beautiful city, there was graffiti and broken windows everywhere. Businesses were boarded up, and you didn't dare leave your home for too long for fear that you would be accosted by the mounting wave of homeless people that had taken over the sidewalks.

With that said I went back to writing my second shorter book to counter the hell "Cancel-Culture" and "Doxing" was wreaking in peoples lives, and I buckled down going to YouTube and Duck Duck Go again to find more truth on what was really going on in our government and larger collective. Out of myself and two Sons, only my youngest Son still watched regular TV programming, and still at that it was always the Main Steam Media News. Gawd how I disliked how they constantly bashed President Trump, but my youngest Son ate it up like candy.

For some reason the only news I could stomach from TV outlets at that time were short news clips on YouTube of FOX TV's Sean Hannity and Tucker Carlson shows. The rest of my information came from alternative sources that I found on YouTube, as I was never a Twitter Fan. I had also learned after my Son's death to curb my addiction to Facebook, and I wasn't on there much now, either. It was then that I attracted a client that was an editor for a major main stream media outlet. She was on the phone with me daily, and when she started to pick up that I wasn't far left liberal leaning, even though my youngest Son was gay, she confronted me about where I was getting my information outside of my Guide Ephraim. When she heard about the shows I watched once in a great while on FOX with Hannity and Carlson she came unglued on me, royally chewing me out with as much shaming as she could possibly throw at me. I will never forget what she told me when I made the truthful statement that there was a growing trend of people no longer wanting to go to TV programming to find out what was happening, or get their entertainment. When my TV editor client heard me say this she stated as if she owned every sovereign bone in my body, "you can't do that, and neither can all those other people!" Wow...it was then that it finally hit home that the CIA's Project Mockingbird was real, and that people that worked for media outlets had been implementing it since before I was born. I haven't been able to take any Main Stream Media news seriously since then.

In August of 2020 my oldest Son and I hugged my youngest Son, as we left our Portland apartment in his charge to go live in a more quiet place in Montana. Now I am fully awake to what is really going on behind the scenes in our government and larger collective systems, along with our banking system, and I currently feel that I live in a whole different world outside of half the US population. In my Montana world we don't wear masks, or feel the need to get injected with an experimental jab that the FDA has not approved of. We don't live in fear, most of us don't watch TV or have any time to watch very much of it, because we are too busy getting into our real lives and community. Between two online businesses, swimming in the river, taking walks in the park with my dog, and riding motorcycles, I don't have any time to focus on all the fear-based lies coming from that box you call a TV, and neither do most of my neighbors. Awe heck...our small mountain town is about as normal and peaceful as the Andy Griffin show! With that said, I'm saddened to say that if you go to our capital and hour and a half away, you will find people all masked and vaccinated up, with proper social distancing, and by golly if you don't do those three things people will call the police on you. Meanwhile myself, along with my two left, liberal leaning Sons, all respect each other and get along great. This is because I understand that they, like almost everyone in America has been programmed by that box we call a TV to think, believe, feel, and behave in a certain patterned way. I also understand that it will take time for them to really understand what really has happened since before they were born, and what is really happening now to undo all the damage that was done by Project Mockingbird and the Deep State Cabal.

So why did I take the time to tell you all of this?

Surely I must be trying to get you to believe the way I do...right?

Sigh...nothing could be further from the truth my dear friend, because this IS NOT about me...this is about **YOU!**

Why my story above is so important to **YOU** is because it shows you in real time a simple...**VERY POWERFUL**...process that you must go through in order to hone your ability to solve your problem. You see from 2016 into the spring of 2021 I allowed my soul and mind to be opened up so that all my grief, soul pain, and old outdated core beliefs could be released. From there, thanks to the help of my business mentor and his team, I set about healing myself, learning to think differently, and resetting what my core beliefs were.

With this said, the "red pill" I am asking you to take **IS NOT** in believing what I have learned in the last four years about the 1% Deep State, Cabal, Satanic cult that has been ruling us (it's slaves) for hundreds of years with an iron fist of debt and mind programming, beginning at childbirth. I don't ask you to believe that they will do whatever it takes to hide the human trafficking that they make more money from more than the drugs they sell to our neighbors and family members. Nor do I ask you to believe that these same people are raping, eating, and making the adrenochrome drug, that they party with, from capturing our family members and children, only to put them through years of horrific ceremonies and vile abusive acts, before they kill them. I don't ask you to listen to the child screams that I heard coming from Harvey Weinstein's laptop, or watch the horrific frazzle-drip video of Hillary Clinton and her aide eating a child while it was still alive. I don't ask you to watch the thousand of documented court testimonial videos of Satanic Abuse Ritual survivors shaking, as they tell the truth what happened to them at the hands of of high level people in our government, churches, big businesses, banking industries, legal system, law enforcement agencies, and most of Hollywood big players. I'm not asking you to believe that our 2020 elections were stolen, as they have been rigged since before I was born in 1970, hence the reason why I have never voted in this lifetime. Yep...not wasting my time until they fix that crooked system. I'm not asking you to believe that income taxes were ruled to be illegal by our Supreme Court. Also with that ruling, both our legislative branches passed a law for all monies taken through income taxes in past years be reversed and given back to the American Citizens, with this being done when President Clinton was in office. I'm not asking you to believe that 911 was perpetrated by our own government to keep themselves from having to implement the repayment of all monies taken American citizens illegally. I'm not asking you to believe that the Federal Swift Banking System has been bankrupted and totally collapsed. I'm not asking you to believe that NESARA/GESARA and the Quantum Financial Banking System is not only real, but also that it has replaced the Federal Swift Banking System, even though every banker at a higher management level will confirm that this to true. I'm not asking you to believe that Americans are going back to living by our original 1776 constitution, and that the good guys, our military, and our Commander and Chief, Donald J. Trump are making sure to get it all done, peacefully behind the scenes. Nope...there is NO WAY IN HELL I AM ASKING YOU TO BELIEVE ANY OF THIS! All of the above is **NOT** the "Red Pill" I am talking about...even though it would help if you would stop watching TV programming long enough to really look into what is REALLY going on around you in your world. I mean really...if you don't like the rules that are being made at a city and county level, then wouldn't it behoove you to show at at council, school board, and/or health board meeting and get involved? I'm just saying...the way these evil 1% people took over every part of our country was by programming the American public thoughts through the TV, slowly integrating and inserting their people into all of our functioning systems, from the local to the federal level, and then extending credit to everyone in order to enslave us all in debt. But...I digress...and again...this is NOT the "Red Pill" that I am talking about!

Naw...the **REAL RED PILL** that I am asking you to swallow are four **VERY IMPORTANT** things that you need you to be aware of, and willing to act on, **BEFORE** you read any further in this book!!!

1. In order for me to be able to help you solve your flaming problem, **you MUST be willing and committed** to helping yourself, and participate in the solving of your said problem!

2. You must be willing to be **open minded** to receiving new, possibly conflicting information, that might not jive with what you already think to be true.

3. You must be willing to **take responsibility** for everything in your life that you have created...good & bad. In other words... you must be willing to be open to learning how **to be sovereign.**

4. You must be willing **to act consistently** on what is being taught in the book, because without the consistent repetition of doing something different...yeh...you're dead in the water on problem solving.

KAPEESH?

Why...you ask?

Simply because I only have the time it takes for you to read this book to clear all of the crap programming that was put into your brain since birth just enough so that you can work with me to solve your looming, eminent problem. With that said let's get one thing straight. I'm not here to blow smoke up your ass with flowery speech. I'm here to get you the results you need to help you solve your damn problem, ok. With that said I have a huge heart of gold in the middle of all these rough edges...so thank you for all your beautiful patience!

This is why I am known as the "Get your head outta your ass" marketer. What can I say...I'm a biker...it fits.

If these four things are not what you want to do in order to hone your problem solving skill-set...

...then it's ok to close this book and give it to the black sheep outcast in your family that thinks for themselves, or someone that is so desperate to have their problem solved that they will actually take these four steps to do so.

Once you give this book away, go back to your usual world of doing the same things over and over again...expecting something different to happen...while claiming your right to complain about things when they don't happen the way you wanted them to, ok.

It's all good though...no judgment here...Go In Peace... :)

CHAPTER 2

Through The Eyes Of A Child

O H...you're still here?!!! Well, I'm really glad that you chose to stick with me, not for my sake, but simply so that we can get down to helping **YOU** out of your jam! So...again...you have a problem...it's not going away...and you need help...right? Now here is the first thing that will probably throw you for a bit of a loop. What is happening right now with you is NOT your REAL problem.

Ehh???

I know what I just said is probably NOT what you want to hear right now, but **IT IS** what you **NEED TO HEAR** right now!

To be brutally honest with you the real crux of the problem that you are having right now lies in your deep seeded core beliefs. Those core beliefs were fully formed and hard-wired into your subconscious brain by the time you were seven years old. Think back to when you were a child. First of all, you were a lot smaller than what you are now. Second, you had parents that were in full control of you life. And third, you had very little life experience.

Believe it or not your brain, even as a grown up adult, is still perceiving the world around you as a small helpless child. Basically, your body and hormones have all changed to bring you into being an adult, but your brain is still stuck in childhood. Even worse, it is now hitting the replay button on all the painful events of your child life, trying to understand what happened and why. This is where 99.99% of your problems are formed, and it is your job to hit the STOP button and not let your brain keep replaying all the painful situations that you lived through as a child! After I tell you how to do this, you can then take the steps to record new programming in your subconscious brain in order to live a happier, more fulfilled life.

Most of us as adults go about our lives completely unaware that we are still seeing everything through the eyes of our inner child self, and this is what trips us up the majority of the time. Having said this, in short, your **REAL PROBLEM** is that you are seeing things in your adult life from your inner child's perspective and core beliefs. You see, once you are able to bring yourself into balance in your present moment...as an adult...well then...you will be able to both see and feel just how powerful you can be!

So with this said, as a small, rather helpless and insecure feeling child, you have formed hard core beliefs based on fear and the need to survive in the world around you. The real problem that you are having now is that you are bringing those core beliefs formed in childhood, reinforced with now dysfunctional and outdated coping behavior, into a fully formed adult body, with way more life experience, and a much greater capacity to create.

I know...you're asking...what does this have to do with the fact that my car is broke down and I don't have the money to fix it...right?

Or...you have a seemingly unrelated problem like this. Well, if you stick with me to the end of this book, I promise you that you will be able to put the pieces of the puzzle together easily. From there you will be on your way to solving your problem, and the headache and heartache that it is causing, ok.

At the end of the day, when you dig deep, the origin of your problem is that you are using childhood core beliefs and coping mechanisms, based on little or no life experience and knowledge, to solve much bigger adult problems that requires much more experience and information to solve. **THAT** my friend is the **REAL PROBLEM** that you are needing to solve, before you can unravel and solve your current problem. The good news is that it is fairly easy to learn and implement my simple process of changing outdated core beliefs. The most difficult part is being really consistent with implementing this simple process that I am about to give to you. But hey...you are worth the time it takes to show up for yourself a little bit each and every day... right? Trust me when I say that this will truly be worth every bit of up to 15 minutes a day focusing on changing outdated core beliefs!

If there is one thing that I have learned in my life, it is that repetition is the key to success. I have seen a ton of that success in my life-time, to the tune of currently making around 20k per month as an Entrepreneur. Hi, my name is Dawn Maree and I started out as an Entrepreneur in 2010. Creating my own wealth was exciting at first, but when I couldn't make the money come in consistently because of fear and deep seeded insecurities, I quit and went back into working to make other people rich. It was all I had known in my life. I was taught from childhood that the proper way to live, the most secure way to live, was to go to a job and earn a paycheck. Being an online business owner seemed scary and way out of my league, so I went back to what I had done for over 40 years...ugghhh...working a dreaded job.

I hated working for other people! First of all, as a powerful empath with extra-sensory perception, coupled with being an introvert, I was always having to work with people I would normally avoid in my private life. Second, I had really good work ethic, yet I never seemed to get the pay raises and recognition that I felt I deserved and earned. Third, and more importantly, no matter how hard I worked I never seemed to have enough money to pay my bills, and still have enough left over to live life comfortably...doing things I loved to do after work. Most of all though, as a single parent, I always felt guilty for not spending enough time with my kids because I had to be away from them to work.

Spending time raising my kids was my top priority. When I finally got fed up to my eyeballs with having to be away from my three amazing sons, that needed me the most, I then shifted from working a job to doing everything I could to find a way to work from home. Unfortunately, I was still faced with the problem of having way more bills than I could possibly earn the money to cover them, even with making base wage and commissions. This was a HUGE PROBLEM, and one my child mind couldn't seem to solve, no matter how much my adult self wanted it to.

Finally, after running away from being an entrepreneur for two years, homeless in Portland, cold and only having $3 to my name, I had to face the obvious. There was no work to be had, and even Day Labor did not have any jobs to send me out on. It was then, after having to go to a food bank, that I surrendered and prayed to God for help. The answer that came back to me was still the same...start your own business...and this time face your fear and trust that everything will be ok. Oh...and don't do business to make money...do business to make at least one person's day better. Not feeling like I really had a choice now, this is exactly what I did, and I haven't stopped making money since!

I have had many problems since then, however, because I was willing to trust, I was shown in simple and easy to understand ways HOW to solve every one of them. This in turn helped me to hone my ability to solve any and all problems, and I would like to share this skill-set with you today. Problem solving is like unraveling a tangled pile of string. Once you find one end, it is then that you can begin to back track it through all the knots, and eventually straighten the whole mess out. It only takes thirty times to makes this simple process a habit, and I promise you that it will be worth every moment that you spend learning how to solve problems by changing your outdated core beliefs.

CHAPTER 3

Identifying Your Core Beliefs

Now that we know that the base of all our frustrations and problems stem from outdated childhood core beliefs and how we perceive the world and situations around us, we need to drill down to being able to identify those outdated core beliefs. I mean really... what does my car breaking down and not having enough money do with all of this...right? You see, our outdated core beliefs hide beneath some of our most serious, and not so serious problems, and if we can identify those first we can not only solve our immediate problem, we can also solve the reason why we attracted that problem to us in the first place! Once we change the settings in our Law Of Attraction to one that is more smooth and peaceful in that core belief area of our lives, then those types of problems don't happen anymore.

With that said, let's use the problem I spoke of above as an example, and drill down to the core beliefs that caused this problem to happen in the first place. So let's say that your car broke down, and you don't have the money to pay to get it fixed. The first outdated core belief is that you don't have enough money and you never will. This outdated core belief was formed when you watched your parents struggle to pay the bills, and you often heard that what you wanted was too expensive for your parents to buy for you. You internalized this constant negative feedback as a child and formed a strong core belief that there is a limited amount of money, and you are not good enough to get a good portion of it. Because of this belief you held on to the feeling of lack all the way through to adulthood, and from there you formed a habit of not saving back money because you didn't seem to make enough to even cover the bills anyway...so it was useless to even try to save any money back for emergencies...right? What better way to relive this outdated childhood core belief then to think you don't have enough money to buy a good solid car, so you buy a used, unreliable car, and are then unpleasantly surprised when it breaks down unexpectedly.

The second outdated core belief that contributed to this problem was that bad things happen when you least expect them, because deep inside you are really not a good person, and because of this life is supposed to be difficult and stressful. This core belief was formed when bad things happened to you in childhood and you felt helpless to protect yourself from these occurrences. This belief was reinforced when as you watched the same situations happen to your parents, and there was nothing that you could do to help them, as you heard them say over and over again, how difficult and hard life was. If your parents were religious you probably also heard that famous verse from the bible about how, "we are born in sin," and that didn't help raise your sense of self worth either. So the second outdated core belief that caused this problem was that you innately are bad from birth because you are human and in order to be good...be better...you must suffer through a difficult life full of unexpected, stressful problems. With that said, so many times we feel unworthy of good things so we buy what we think will just get us by instead of really going for creating what we REALLY want...and instead we keep reliving the pain of there being nothing good in life because we ourselves are not good. We truly believe that life is out to break us at a souls core level because we are so bad.

If no one is stepping up to help you with your broke down car, there is one more outdated core belief that has contributed to this problem. That core belief is that because you innately are not a good, deserving person, this means that no one really cares about you or truly loves you unconditionally. This core belief was formed in child-hood because often times parents struggle with their own problems when they are raising children, and that means this happened with your parents, too. This in turn diverted their attention away from you, and on to their own problems. This translated into a world where that you didn't get the emotional support or attention that you needed as a child, giving you a sense of emotional abandonment. To put it bluntly, you were left to fend for yourself, and you carried the pain of that all the way into your adult life, constantly creating the same situations of people never being there for you when you need them the most.

So do you see how I broke that problem down to all of the outdated underlying core beliefs that contributed to you creating the huge problem of your car breaking down and you not having enough money to fix it? Problems are never surface level situations, they are a direct reflection of what is going on in both our thinking, and our souls. When you can get down to the core level of how you created your problem, it is then that you can both solve your problem, **AND** stop them from ever happening again!

CHAPTER 4

What Is Your Problem?

In order to solve your problem, first you must know what a problem actually is. To put it simply a problem happens when a a situation or task comes into your awareness and your brain doesn't have enough information to deal with it efficiently, or complete the task without experiencing difficulty. At the first onset of this awareness fear usually sets in immediately, amplifying our discomfort to a level that causes us to focus more on the fear and the problem, and less on solving the problem.

When fear sets in, like a blinding fog, as all of our negative thinking and fear based questions are activated. Now our problem is amplified even more! What if people think I'm a failure? What if I get hurt? What if I die from this? What if my good reputation is ruined? What if people think I'm a bad person now? What if I'm going to jail? What if I lose everything I've worked so hard for? What if I lose my job? What if I lose my health? What if I lose my loved ones? And... the list goes on and on...and on.

Well...by now you are the proud owner of a gynormous problem and you have just created it in record time! I know...I know...you are really bugged and irritated that I keep saying, "problem you created," simply because to you it seems as if you had **NOTHING** to do with your problem that came to you, unexpected, out of nowhere, and with it the ruining of your whole day, possibly your whole week or month, and on rare occasion...your life...right? You are the victim here and I should feel empathy and compassion for you. How dare I be so judgmental and think you had anything to do with creating your own problem...**SHEESH!!!**

Well for one I am just stating a fact based on energetic flow and quantum physics. Two, I really do care about that fact that your problem is painful, stressful, and difficult for you...that's the whole reason I am taking the time to write this book. And three, I have walked many miles in your shoes and I know exactly how painful and frustrating problems can be. With that said let's give you more information so that you can solve your problem as quick as possible, ok!

On the surface your problem seems huge and unsolvable...right? Your mate left you for someone else. Your loved one died. You have a huge bill hanging over your head and you don't have the money to pay it. You made a huge mistake at work and you might get fired. You over-indulged in some way and now you look like an utter asshole. You just got in a car wreck. And again...the list of possible problems are infinite, however the fact still remains that the answer to solving your problem, which are in truth is only symptoms of your REAL CORE problem, in a fast and easy way, is to go deeper than just the surface level.

But WAIT...first you must recognize that you do have a problem, and dismantle any fear and fear based thoughts around the initial surface part of the problem!!! Below are the steps to take to dismantle your fear.

1. Take time to take deep breaths and get oxygen to your brain so that the fear fog clears up.

2. From there go into releasing pent up emotion without projecting it at anyone, or any living thing. (Pound on the steering wheel, if you're alone let off a stream of obscenities that would make a sailor proud, work out aggressively, scream into a pillow, pound on the bed with a baseball bat, put your head down and allow yourself to cry, curl up on your bed with your favorite pillow and cry, etc.)

3. If you have enough time, before trying to do anything to solve your problem allow yourself to sleep for a bit, and before going to sleep ask your Creator Parents (God, Source, Allah, Buddha...etc.) to help you solve your problem. If there is no time to sleep still be bold enough to ask for help before attempting to solve your problem.

4. Last but not least, if you don't have time to sleep on your problem, make sure to clear you mind of negative thoughts. Then, reassure yourself that everything is going to be ok, and that things will all work out even better than you can imagine right now, because you have solved problems before, and by doing this more and more, you are getting better and better at it each and every time you solve a problem.

5. Speak gratitude into your heart, that your problem has created an opportunity to learn something new, and to increase your

ability to trust in yourself, the Universe, and your Creator Parents (God, Source, Allah, Buddha...etc.)

6. Make sure to reassure yourself that it doesn't matter what anybody else thinks, simply because you love, forgive, and accept yourself.

*It would be helpful to write the above steps down!

For example, one time within three seconds flat, I found that I had been thrown down to the floor on my back, and I had a 180lb full-grown, ex-con man, that could easily bench 350lbs, straddling me, while he used both of his hands to choke me out, in an attempt to kill me. Needless to say, this was a huge problem that I really did not have time to think about. I had never been in a fight before, as I was punished severely as a child if I was to even show anger, let alone get in a fight. With this said, my attempts to fight this man trying to kill me were futile to it's core, but I was able to relax enough for just a few seconds to stop my thoughts and scream in my head, GOD HELP ME!

The moment the last word left my screaming brain, time slowed down, and a thought told me to reach up and grab the man's wind pipe, squeeze as hard as I could with me fingers, and crush it. I did what the voice in my head told me to do, and right before I crushed his windpipe, the man jumped off of me. From there a blind rage took over my body as I screamed, jumped to my feet, and ran to the stairs to go up and out of the door.

Even before I could reach the second step the man caught up with me, threw me against the wall, and once again commenced with his plans to choke me out and kill me. This time the voice in my head told me to reach for his man parts and do as much damage as I could.

When the man saw the rage in my eyes and my hands reaching for his soft spot to rip it up, he jumped off of me again, as I stormed up the stairs at lightening speed, screaming in rage the whole way. Needless to say, I won that fight, and both the symptom of a man trying to kill me, and my core level problem of believing that men could always hurt or kill me, was solved. From that moment on I had set a new updated core belief that I was no longer a victim, and that I could win any fight...with ANYONE...and that included very big men!

I had been through so much abuse at the hands of men as a helpless child, that as an adult I did not realize that I could now fight a man and win. After winning that fight for my life with a man, I took my power back and signed up to take jujitsu, and karate classes to further hone my fighting skills. I have never been afraid of a man again, and because my terror of men hurting and/or killing me is gone, I no longer attract angry aggressive men.

Now, my second example of having a problem is way different from that of first one. My second problem was one where I wanted to start my own successful online business, and it cost $1,500 to get mentoring from the business mentor that I wanted. The was a rather large problem for me because I was at a point in life where I was barely able to make ends meet. This was because I had a Son that was on the verge of dying, and all of my money went to keeping him out of crisis and alive. Besides this, I had never been able to manifest a larger sum of money, like the one I needed now, very easily. I only knew how to work for money, and I needed more information on how to "attract" money to me easily, without having to take the time to "work" for it. This is where I went through all the steps I listed above, only I took it a step further in being diligent to change the mindset and my core beliefs around money, and mostly the lack of it! Within a week, out of the blue, my PayPal business account offered me a loan for that exact amount of $1,500 that I needed.

My Son ended up dying three months after I got the PayPal business loan and bought the business mentoring that I needed, but not before he got see my first big ticket sale! I remember everything about that day as I turned my computer around to show him that I had made over $400 in one sale. I can also remember very vividly seeing in his eyes that he finally knew his Mom would be just fine when it came to having enough money.

You see when steps 1-6 above are taken to clear negative emotions and thoughts around a problem that arises, it is then that you will find that your ability to think becomes more objective and clear. Once the negative emotions and thoughts are gone, you are then able find and access the information that you are needing in a much easier manner in order to solve your problem. Just to be clear, problem solving comes in 3 phases. Phase 1 is clearing all the negative emotions and thoughts in the onset of the problem. Phase 2 is changing your outdated childhood core beliefs and feelings around the problem. Phase 3 is gathering all the information that you will need to solve your problem with peace and ease.

With that said, my immediate problems were not really the problem at all, they were only symptoms of my real problem. My REAL problem was that I didn't have enough information to deal with each situation, and my outdated core beliefs were blocking me from creating the solutions I needed at that moment. Most of the time what we THINK the problem is, is only a surface SYPMTOM of the REAL core level problem that we are having. Once you get the SYPMTOMS out of the way then you can ease into gathering facts and information so that you can solve your problem at both a surface, AND a core level. Without all of the fear, and fear based emotions in the way this process of information gathering and learning, problem solving can be quite fun if you allow yourself to see it that way.

Now that we have that first preliminary simple process of clearing the SYMPTOMS of your problem out of the way...we can now get into solving your problem at a core level. Remember now, we create problems by bringing outdated core beliefs that we have formed in childhood into our adult lives. With this said, let's go into some of the most common core beliefs that we bring from childhood into our adult lives. Many of these core beliefs, will cause serious problems, and even death, if we don't pay attention to them and make a serious, consistent effort to change them.

CHAPTER 5

I Am Stupid

If you only knew how many times I have beat myself up and berated myself in my head for doing something I deem...stupid...and I'll lay odds that if you are still reading this book that you do the same thing. We truly and honestly believe, as adults, that we are not intelligent enough, and because of this, we must suffer for the rest of our lives. Where does this core belief come from?

It comes from being punished and/or shamed for making mistakes as children. My parents were religious, and their favorite verse to repeat said, "spare the rod, spoil the child." Believe it or not there are a lot of you reading this book that still genuinely believe that verse to be gospel truth, and you swear by it. I mean isn't what's wrong with the world today caused by parents not spanking their kids enough? I'm not saying your are wrong or right...and I am not judging you in anyway...but did you stop to question what was taught to you as a child and prove it out for yourself?

Growing up in a supposed "Christian" commune, I didn't have a chance in hell, as all the up to 135 members, deeply believed in that verse. I was spanked, beat, what ever you want to call it, with anything the adult close to me could get their hands, on almost every day of my child life until I was around 9 years old, whether I made a mistake or not. I was put under ice cold showers, stood in corners for long periods of time, publicly shamed and humiliated. I was also told that I was stupid, that I was a slut, and a whore, and I was never allowed to see my friends outside of school...all for making mistakes. Is it any wonder why I would form a hard core belief in childhood that I was stupid? I mean, I must have been stupid because I was making so many mistakes...right?

Oh....in case you still don't believe that I'm not not judging you...I was taught to parent the same way by my parents. I did this because I was still desperately trying to gain my own parents approval and acceptance. I went against everything I promised myself, after suffering through years of childhood abuse, that I would never do with my children. Sadly as I went along with my parents advise and demands for me to physically discipline my own children, I felt absolutely horrible every time I did it. Inside of me I knew I was doing something that was hurting both myself and my children, but between my parents and thousands of people around me in the Christian community, the need to be accepted outweighed the need to be true to myself and my children. With that said, I really do understand why people believe so staunchly in physically disciplining their children, because at one point I did too, I just wish to this day that I had parented differently according to how I felt inside that I should parent.

It was only when I finally started keeping my commitment to myself to heal deeper soul injuries consistently, that I truly understood the damage that I had done to my own children in not being true to how I felt I was supposed to parent my them. As a young single parent

I could still remember all the pain of the abuse I went through as a child, and I still went against my knowing that I shouldn't physically discipline my own children, even if I did make sure to be ultra careful never to be verbally or emotionally abusive. To this day I am still releasing guilt around what I did to my own children in the name of supposedly loving them, when in reality I was just projecting all of my fear, anger, and frustration at them for not doing what I wanted them to do, and what I thought was right for them.

I was told my children would love and respect, and trust me more if I physically discipline them more, when it actually did just the opposite. It made them feel that their world was unsafe, that it was not acceptable to show any type of emotion, that they were somehow bad, and imperfect, and most of all that it was not acceptable to make mistakes. I am still working patiently with the two that are left alive in their adult years to correct those childhood core beliefs that I instilled in them early on in their lives. I don't do this out of guilt anymore, I do it because I have a good relationship with myself now, and I am showing them how to do the same for themselves by example. Lately I have come to a place of surrender where I don't judge others for how they parent their own children, let alone myself anymore, and this brings me much more peace.

Did I learn a better way to raise my kids without physically disciplining them?

You bet!

I let them feel their emotions, yet my answer stays the same, if I know I am right in guiding them. I am no longer ashamed to stand near a kicking and screaming kid in public, and wait for them to work through the emotion...while my answer stands to be the same. I do loving restraint now in keeping my children from personal harm or harming others. I take away privileges until they are ready to listen to me and do what I say. I give them ways to release their negative emotions without projecting them at others, i.e. let them hit the bed mattress with a plastic wiffle bat, punch a punching bag, scream into a pillow, or give them a special pillow or stuffed animal to curl up and cry into. I actively listen to my children. I apologize when I make a parenting mistake. Finally, I am open to learning from my children, and in our house it is ok for me to change my mind if I receive new information that supports what it is that my children want in a good way. Debate is encouraged as well as showing emotions, objectivity is praised and encouraged, as well as empathy, and compassion, reciprocity, reading...oh...and we do a lot of hugs. :) Respect is given and received, trust is earned in our home, mistakes are met with compassion, and my adult children and I have built a stronger bond than we could have ever imagined. With this said I am NOT saying that this is how you should parent. What I AM SAYING is that you should parent according to how YOU FEEL is right, and it would be helpful to NOT let anyone tell you otherwise.

There are other ways that we develop a core belief that we are stupid in childhood, like getting held back in school, being ridiculed for having a disability, not fitting in with the other children in school enough, being bullied, having to endure verbal and emotional abuse, and the list goes on and on.

The simple fact remains that making mistakes is the main way that humans learn. We learn in other ways also, like from watching others, and from going to school. Regardless though, we tend to remember the lessons we learn from making mistakes much more simply because usually there is discomfort, and often pain involved when we learn from mistakes. We, for the most part, do not like pain, so our memory tends to be very good when it comes to avoiding it by all costs! When we can remove the shame and guilt emotions around making mistakes, it is then that we can fast-track our learning process, and stop creating problems based on trying to resolve the issues around making mistakes and feeling stupid about it.

One more thing here...we often think that if we learn differently than other people...then this must surely mean that we are stupid. Nothing could be further from the truth! Some of the people that I know with the highest IQ's, that also have extra-sensory perception, must have hands on training in order to learn effectively, simply because their body must be in movement in order to learn something new. These are the same people that cannot sit in a classroom, however, they still love to read. They cannot sit to meditate but they can do walking meditation and come up with answers to complex problems in short periods of time.

My hair dresser, who is around sixty years old, told me that if anyone tries to teach her about computer or tech related things, that her brain literally aches, and hurts. Yet when it comes to intuiting answers to complex business or social problems, she is highly accurate, and can solve those problems at lightening speed. Her husband, on the other hand, who is a little older than her, can understand everything about computers, cell phones, and anything techie. Solving problems when it comes to the tech department is something that he prides himself on being a genius at, yet when it comes to social and business problems he hides from them, and thinks that he is stupid when it comes to solving those types of problems.

With that example given, do you see why just because you may learn differently, you are NOT stupid?

I mean really...you were intelligent enough to get through enough life to pick up this book and read it...I guarantee that you can learn anything that intrigues you enough, or that you are passionate enough about. Most of the lack of being able to learn when it comes down to brass tacks, is that people **HATE** learning about things that bore them. Knowing this, it would be helpful if you find yourself faced with having to learn about something critical that bores you, that you find another way of learning about it that isn't quite so boring...like on-the-job training, instead of classroom learning. Just know though, at the end of the day you ARE truly intelligent, simply because you are human, and our only purpose as human beings here in this life on earth is to learn more, do more, and BE MORE...so let's get to it, ok!

CHAPTER 6

There Is Not Enough For Me

How many times do you remember seeing your parents stress and/or argue over paying bills? How many times were you told that your parents didn't have the money to get what you wanted, or that you had to wait for it because your parents had to save money back for it. How many times did you daydream as a child of going to a toy store to buy anything you wanted, only because nothing could be farther from the truth in your real life. How many times were you aware of food shortages as a child because of lack of money. How many times have you heard from you parents, others close to you, or from the T.V., that we are going to run out of money, trees in the forests, water, or other natural resources? How many times did you hear growing up that money was the root of all evil, and to be rich was to be selfish and bad?

Well, if you identified with even a few of those questions above then there is a high probability that you formed a core belief in childhood that there was never enough for you, and there never would be. That only a very few rich people lived an abundant life, and because your parents were not rich that this in some way made you less than everyone else, and you could never be rich in your lifetime...unless you from some stroke of luck, won the lottery!

I am so sorry to break the news to you, however, you were programmed since the time you entered the school system to learn what you needed to know in order to land a good job, and then go to work for someone else to make them wealthy. You were not taught to create your own wealth by being in business for yourself in school! You were not taught to think about or be a business owner, you were taught to WORK for a business owner, because gawd forbid that you come to know your REAL power as a creator on a grand scale. If you landed a good job, you were taught that buying all the things you wanted on credit was the way to be accepted and fit in with all the good outstanding people, and that this was happiness...right?

So, here you are, up to your ears in debt, going to a job that you either hate, or tolerate, but at the end of the day you would rather be doing something else, and you're still not happy. Oh...and you still don't have enough money to cover all the bills, or enough time to spend with loved ones. Why is this? Well you say, it's because money is the root of all evil and I didn't listen to that caution when I was growing up...that's why! No...not really...it's because you were taught that both you and money are bad and that couldn't be further from the truth.

So let's break this down to where you can understand the error in that core belief. Money is an energy like water or electricity. You can use it to help yourself live a life with less stress because you have money to pay for everything you need and want, and also help others out with it, too. Or...you can use money to do harmful things to yourself and others, like pay for drugs and alcohol, or hire a hit-man to kill someone. However, at the end of the day money is not the true root of evil, it is how a human chooses to use it that makes it negative or positive in it's usage. Oh...and you dear friend, at a soul core level... are pure positive energy, so in truth there is really nothing bad about you. In human form you are truly perfect in your imperfection because this is how you are learning to do more, and be more.

Now let's talk about the "never enough" part of money. Again, money is an energy like water, there is NO LACK of it on the earth plane. Just like water is recycled over and over again, from the earth to the clouds, and back down to the earth again, money is an infinite energy. Why? Because money can be made out of ANYTHING! It can be made out of precious metals, paper, precious stones, crypto currency (computers), or anything that can be traded for something other people want. With that said, there in never a LACK of money, we are only lacking information on how to get, and/or attract more money, more effortlessly, and more consistently, within in a shorter period of time.

With that said, all you really need in order to solve your problem of not ever having enough money is more information on how to attract and manifest money, instead of working hard for it. I know...I know...you were taught that if you didn't work hard for your money that you would not know the value of things, and you would become self-centered and selfish...right? Well, I'm not sorry to tell you that this was also a core belief taught to you to keep you from growing into the magnificent power of being able to create from inside of you, through your beliefs and thoughts, coupled with your emotions (energy-in-motion). In reality, the more money that you have, coupled with the less fear you have, works out to you having less stress in your life. This in turn has the effect on you focusing more in the well-being of the world and others around you in a less self-centered place. When you know how to create money effortlessly, you tend to be more giving and less selfish and afraid of never getting the money back.

I remember that when I didn't know how to attract or manifest money more easily, I used to always have to be on a budget for my groceries and bills, because I felt that when the money was gone, that there was no more. Life is so different for me now that I know how to manifest and attract money in my businesses, instead of "working hard" for it. I don't live by a budget anymore, I don't look at price tags as much anymore, I give more to others in need, and I am aware of their needs more often. Best of all, I have more money in my savings account than ever before because it doesn't cross my mind anymore that I can't get more money easily, if I run out of it.

You see at the end of the day attracting and manifesting money is a skill-set that humans learn, and true to everything we learn, once we learn it we can never forget how to do it. This means that for every outdated core belief that I change into a more positive core belief, based on who I am now as an adult, I increase my capacity to feeling more positive emotions more of the time, which in turn increases the amount of money that I am able to manifest and attract. It really is a simple process that once put in motion and thoroughly committed to, it is easy to implement daily, and the results are absolutely phenomenal! Well...at least for me they have been as I have never in my life been able to make 20k a month, like I do now.

CHAPTER 7

I Am Not Good Enough

O k, now we are on a roll, so let's roll into the next outdated core belief that is the root cause of most of the problems in our lives. This belief is one where we believe and feel at a core level that we are bad, and in this that we are not good enough for good people and good things to happen in our lives. This belief was formed in childhood when hurtful things would happen to us as children and our parents would tell us that this was because we had misbehaved and we were bad. Even if we had not misbehaved then there was still nothing that they could do about the hurtful things that happened. When as children we constantly watched our own parents play a victim role in life, it caused us to feel helpless, bad, and like we were not good enough to bring goodness to ourselves or our family.

I remember one time I begged my Mom to not leave the commune to go on another trip with the Founder because I was being neglected and abused, and she left anyway, leaving me with a home-made life size doll in her place. It was a low point in my life as a child. I felt like I was not good enough for my own Mother to want to stay home to love and protect me, and in this I definitely did not deserve her love. My Mother was always leaving my brother and I at the commune, to be looked after by others, while she traveled with and took care of the Founder on road trips. I did not know that she had also been talked into having an affair with him. As a child I don't remember being hugged or held by my Mom, or by any other woman that took care of me when my mother wasn't at the commune, and the only time men showed me affection was usually for sexual reasons, and this terrified me. It was at this point that point I formed a hard core belief that not only was I not good enough to be anyone's child, I was also dirty, broken, ugly, fat, and unlovable because of all the neglect and abuse that I had gone through.

I know clients that form the same core belief of not being good enough or lovable simply because their parents went through a divorce. The logic behind this was that if the child had been good enough then they could have kept their family together. Even though every adult knows that this is not anywhere near the truth, a child going through the traumatic change of a break-up in their family sees things quite differently. The difficulty comes in when that core belief gets drug into adulthood, and the person still perceives themselves as not good enough and unlovable. This also happens when a parent dies, or the child suffers through abuse and neglect, as I did.

The problems that we create around this outdated core belief can be catastrophic at times. Anytime we create something really good, like a larger lump sum of money, our perfect job, a new house, or our perfect mate, it is at that point that the outdated core belief of not being good enough and unlovable kicks in, and we subconsciously go into over-drive in self-sabotaging whatever good we created. We do this because consciously we don't have enough information on how to heal the pain created in our souls in childhood that caused this outdated core belief to be formed, and eventually our subconscious is successful at sabotaging the good we created. When this happens it reinforces the outdated core belief and feeling inside of us that we are truly not enough and in that we are unlovable.

The self-sabotaging problems show up in situations where we spend money so fast that we end up poor and penniless, while other times we pick fights with our mates because we don't feel worthy of their goodness and love. Still other problems are ones where we get behind on our mortgage and we can't catch up on the payments, or the note is sold to a lender that swindles the house right out of our possession. We make mistakes at work because we are so afraid of losing our job. We stress so much about pregnancies that we cause ourselves to miscarry. We look down for a second at our phone and wreck our brand new car. We worry so much about being alone that we focus on our own unworthiness, hate ourselves even more, and then complain about not being able to get a date...and the list goes on and on.

Do you see where I'm going with this? The simple truth is that you are not bad, you were never bad, hurtful things happened in your childhood that had no reflection on who you were or are as a human being. For every pain that you have felt, there is a capacity in you to heal it, learn from it, and expand in your soul's with more compassion and understanding to be stronger, better, and more amazing than what you were before. In true reality you are pure positive energy in a dense human body, and you came to earth to learn more, do more, create more, and be more...KAPEESH?

CHAPTER 8

I Can't Trust

This outdated childhood core belief is one that still makes me wince a bit to this day. This core belief is formed in childhood when you end up being hurt most by the adults in your life that are supposed to protect and love you the most. Most of the time these adults are family members, but sometimes they are also people in authority positions like teachers, policemen, doctors, and clergymen.

What's interesting about this core belief is that a child loses the ability to trust when many people close to them betray their trust, and/or even if just one adult does it. They can also form this belief if they are constantly hurt by adults close to them, and/or again, even if they have only been hurt just once by an adult they look up to and trust. When a child is betrayed and hurt by an adult close to them that they trust, whether it be physically, verbally, emotionally, or sexually, their essence of pure innocence leaves and fear takes it's place. It is at that moment that a child's life is changed forever in a way where they will always have a sense of fear from then on, and their sense of innocence begins to fade away.

What's worse is that you probably can't remember all the good things that adult's close to you did for you in childhood, but you can remember every time that they betrayed and hurt you. This caused you to be hyper-vigilant in looking out for future occurrences of being possibly hurt by adults again as a child, and soon your focus was consumed with avoiding adults that would hurt you and not so much on playing and being carefree anymore. Sure, you still played as a child, but not as much now that you felt like you had to look out for and protect yourself.

To make matters even worse. when it comes to being hurt in childhood by adults, often times the adults will put the blame for how they hurt the child back on to the child. How many times have we been told as a child that our bad behavior is what caused our parents to whoop our butts, or how our not doing what we were told caused some type of personal injury to us. I remember being nine years old and telling my caretaker that I was being sexually abused by our commune founder's Son. I was so tired of the abuse that I had finally mustered up enough courage to say something just to make it stop. Afterwards after being publicly shamed by having to repeat my story to eight elders, both male and female, I was made to stand in a dark room to await their judgment. After the elders came out of the meeting, I then had an elder dump a glass of cold water over my head as I was coldly told to, "never do that again."

I also remember one time when my Mother took me out for ice cream. I was so excited that my own Mom wanted to spend time with me that I jumped at the chance to go. I thought at this point that everything would be ok, that I could finally trust my Mom because she really did care about me! Half way through our treat time my heart dropped into my toes as I heard her ask me if my Step-Dad had ever been sexual with me, and she wanted to know about all of the people who had sexually abused me. I still wanted to believe that I could trust my Mother so much that I was completely honest with her about EVERYTHING. Two hours later she had repeated everything I had said to my Step-Dad, which resulted in a beating for me by my Step-Dad. To tell you the truth, the beating from my Step-Dad didn't hurt, it was the betrayal of my own Mother that tore my heart to pieces, and it wasn't the first or last time that this happened.

When a child's trust is betrayed by adult and they are hurt by them, then in turn they are blamed for it, this is when the child also loses trust in themselves. We beat ourselves up in our heads, even as children, and wonder why we didn't see it coming, and why we didn't do more to protect ourselves. The feeling of being alone and having to fend for, and protect ourselves is overwhelming, as we do our best to compensate for our small body size in a world of much bigger and stronger adults. The saddest moment about forming the core belief as a child that we cannot trust, is when we deem ourselves so bad... so unworthy...that we cannot even trust own own selves.

After speaking to thousands of clients over the years, I have found that another source of trust issues in childhood are created around a trusted adult not keeping their word to the child, whether they do or do not have control of the situation in which they made the promise. I have seen children sit on a porch until after dark waiting for a parent that died to come home. At the same time, I have dealt with equal pain in clients who were promised big items as children, with the adults they trusted never being able to deliver on that promise. It would also be helpful to not judge your pain of not being able to trust any less than someone else's pain, because the situation in which it was created wasn't as extreme as others were. All soul pain is traumatic to a child, especially when they set limiting strong core beliefs from it.

It would be helpful to understand that the ability to trust begins with being able to trust ourselves, and also our ability to trust our Creator Parents (Source, God, Allah, Buddha, etc). I know a ton of people that don't believe in humans having a soul, and especially don't believe in the idea that we have Creator Parents that brought our human souls and bodies into existence. For those I will say that I respect your beliefs, so at least start with being committed to yourself in a way where you can begin to feel that trust you have in yourself. If you want to believe that you have Creator Parents, but can't quantify them with your conscious brain and five senses, then do what I did... ask them to make themselves "REAL" to you here on the earth plane. Trust me when I say that if you ask this knowing that there will be an answer...well...you'll see...you will really get an answer.

Once you set a baseline that something bigger than you exists outside of your five senses, and that you can trust this Benevolent Being(s), then you can begin to trust even more, bit by bit, as they prove themselves to be trustworthy. I mean really, why would we have a Universal Law Of Faith, if we didn't have Creator Parents and a loving Universe that we really can trust...right? At the end of the day though, it is only when we surrender and actually practice trust that we are able to prove out whether we can or cannot trust our Creator Parents, and also ourselves. Once you are able to live in and feel trust, it then becomes your reality to the point where you are able to attract people to you that you can also trust.

CHAPTER 9

Something Bad Happens

So there you are, going about your normal routine in your day, when out of the blue someone leaves you a voicemail. It is a cop from another county informing you that your Son is in the hospital and that you need to get there ASAP! Three days later you walk out of the hospital in stunned shock, without your Son, because he died 30 minutes ago. For the umpteenth millionth time it seems like life has just gut punched you out of nowhere, and your left reeling in pain from it.

This actually happened to me, and the question that I get the most from my clients is, "do you see anything in my future that I need to worry about?" Wow, I must have heard that same question in different forms at least one hundred times in the last month! Every time I hear it I cringe, and I do my best to steer people to looking at WHY they asked that particular question. After the experience I had above, I can honestly say that if I knew how my Son was going to die the way he did, I would have put myself in harms way to stop it, and both my Son and I would be dead right now, leaving my two other children without a mother. In hindsight I am really grateful that I didn't see it coming, as it helped me to stay in the present moment to deal with everything just as it played out.

With this said I know from actual life experience also, that when we constantly focus on something that we are afraid of happening, **we create it**, even it we DON'T want it to happen! How does this happen you say? Anytime we put focus on our thoughts we cause them to grow energetically. When we mix feelings (emotion) in with the thoughts we are focused on, that is when we bring our thoughts into the physical world. This is called "manifesting." In simple terms, this is how humans create. Worry is when you mix the emotion of fear with your thoughts, and if you do this long enough, you WILL create what you are worried about. This is why telling someone you are worried about them is NEVER a loving thing to say or do!

Regardless, this question of always asking for information on future bad events that might happen, stems from a childhood core belief that bad things happen unexpectedly, and if we don't see those events coming then we are helpless to protect ourselves from harm. We form this belief when hurtful unexpected events happen to us as children, and because we are smaller than adults we are not only caught off guard in shock, we tend to suffer more trauma because we didn't see it coming. When this happens we feel that things happened this way because we are intrinsically bad at a core level, and/or that we did something wrong to deserve it, or that we didn't do enough to stop the bad event from happening. Regardless, at the end of the day, as a child, we blame ourselves for the hurtful events that happen to us.

When we form this childhood core belief that life is out to crush and harm us with unexpected harmful events, we feel that if we can see it bad things coming, then we can do whatever it takes to avoid them. The problem with this seemingly good problem solving capacity is that we are perceiving that life is happening TO us, instead of the reality that WE have or are CREATING the events in our lives at a soul level from inside of us. As children, once we have been hurt either physically or emotionally we set a baseline of fear that never goes away. Once this baseline is formed it is then that we begin attracting everything to us that we are afraid of, so that through experience we will learn not to fear.

There is another reason why we get hurt unexpectedly in childhood. You see, before we ever come into our physical bodies, we plan out events that will play out in our lives, and we make contracts with people who agree to be a part of our lives on earth. It is called our life blueprint, or more commonly known as our "destiny." Some of the events that we plan to experience in our new child lives on earth are written in to clear karmic debts, for errors that we made in another life. For instance, say that you were a serial killer in the life before this one that killed a lot of women and children. In order to clear all the hurt and damage you had done in that life, and know how it felt to be hurt the way you had hurt other people, there would be a high likelihood that in this life you would have chosen to be a victim of extreme abuse and/or murder. Clearing karmic debts like this allows a human soul to grow in wisdom and compassion in a greater capacity than any other way.

Do you see why the core belief that we develop in childhood that life is hard because bad things happen unexpectedly, and we as victims, need to be on the lookout for these feared events is in error? It was our own soul that planned these events, and in reality life is not the boogey man that we make it out to be. In reality we really

ARE the authors of our own destiny! Our Creator Parents, and the loving Universe filled with opposite polarity energy, that they allow us to come to, is here to support us and help us create expansion and growth in our souls as much as we possibly can in a life-time.

With this said though, after we create our life destiny blueprint, before we incarnate into our physical bodies, we do a clean sweep of our memory so that we forget everything we planned coming into our bodies. This way we can learn our lessons with real emotional energy so that we don't ever forget what we learn in our life-time. We also choose to forget so that we can make new permanent memories in real time here on earth in our new life. We do this because when it comes to tangible infinite treasure that we can actually take with us going back into our spirit bodies, those priceless treasures are memories gained, truth assimilated, and compassionate energy earned.

This is why changing outdated childhood beliefs is so important. We make our first set of core beliefs and hard set them by the time we are seven years old. Needles to say, we create them on limited information and then expect those core beliefs to carry us through a life-time smoothly, not accounting for soul growth in wisdom, discernment, higher development, and compassion. Not only that, if we base our behavior and how we relate to the world around us based on limited core beliefs, this is where old meets new and the two don't mix or fit together well.

CHAPTER 10

I Am Alone

The outdated core belief that you are alone is by far the scariest one to face and change. We develop the core belief as children in two different ways. First, we are physically left alone a lot to fend for ourselves. Second, the adults that are responsible for our care may be around us a lot, however, they pay very little attention to us as children, leaving us to believe that in truth we are, for the most part a ghost, and really alone.

As children we usually unconditionally love the adults that care for us so much that we tend to idolize them, and when they abandon us, at this point our young brains think that it must be our own fault. We were too ugly, too fat, too skinny, we wanted too much, we didn't do things right, we didn't help as much as we should have, we were so bad that we hurt the missing person, we didn't try hard enough to keep them around, etc. Once this gets etched in our child brains, it sticks like gorilla glue because it is cemented in with the emotions of terror, fear, rejection, and shame.

I remember at the tender age of less than a year old, my Mom and Dad had gotten a divorce and all of the sudden, my Dad was gone. To make matters worse, two and a half years later after not being able to force myself to go to sleep at nap-time, I was being punished by being dumped on the side of a dirt road, way out in rolling wheat fields as far as the eye could see, and left me there to scream in terror as I watched my mother and caretaker drive out of sight. All I could think of was how I was going to be bitten by snakes and eaten alive by coyotes and bears. My tiny body shook with so much horror that I couldn't move. After what seemed like an hour my Mom and caretaker came back to pick me up, however, not after I had firmly formed a core belief that at some point, everyone I loved or got close to, would leave me alone to fend for myself.

After this the abandonment only became worse, and although there were anywhere between 88-135 people around me all of the time, I felt like a walking ghost. No one wanted to play with me, no one hugged me or reached out to spend time with me. Most of all, the only time I got attention was to be disciplined for things I did wrong. It wasn't long before I stopped wanting anybodies attention simply because it usually involved some type of sexual, emotional, or physical pain.

You see as I experienced above, the real damaging belief around abandonment happening when we are children, is that we come to expect that when people we like, love, and trust come into our lives, they are going to leave and we are helpless in feeling the pain the ensues afterwards. One way that we as children try to cope with this pain of people leaving us is to either stay away from people we like and love, or misbehave so that they won't want to be around us.

Now look at how we take that core belief and behavior into adult life. Do you get why we can't commit to someone in a relationship, why we pick fights with them, and we ghost and bread-crumb them? These are but a few of the dysfunctional coping behaviors that we develop around the core belief that people will always leave us, and that in this we are alone. Does it make this ok for us as adults to behave this way? HELL NO...but we do it anyway out of a sheer need to not be hurt emotionally and at a soul level anymore. The most difficult thing to believe around all of this is that as adults, WE are the ones that keep recreating this hurtful problem of abandonment in relationships, because we never understood why it happened to us as children, and as adults we keep trying to fix what went wrong.

Even worse, we recreate this abandonment problem as adults, by either becoming promiscuous, needing someone in our bed at all times, or we become cynical hermits that hide in our houses, only to live our entire social lives in a small box we call a computer or cell phone. If we become promiscuous we tend to suffer from mental and health problems, and/or society judges us and we end up being shunned for it all. If we become cynical hermits, at first the tendency to hide from the world feels good because we don't have a lot of human emotional messiness around us, but in the end we tend to feel isolated and miserable in that self isolation. Unfortunately, after a longer period of time either imbalance tends to hurt our soul even more because we are now lacking on good health mentally and physically, human touch, affection, and in person interaction and we feel more alone than ever!

Are we in reality really alone? That is the question that we need to answer in order to be able to change the outdated childhood belief that we are alone. The real truth behind that question is that...no...we are never really ever alone.

Why is this you ask? Simply because human beings are made up of both physically dense matter in our bodies, and also pure energy, somewhat like electricity, only different and more powerful in their spirit bodies and souls. In fact, every living thing on earth is made up of the same base core energy that makes up a human being and the only difference is that a human being has a soul, and the rest of creation does not. Because of this, we has humans live in a world where we are not only connected in a very close way with the world in which we live, we are also surrounded by other people in spirit form (pure energy form) that are helping us on the earth place 24/7 around the clock. To top it off, we have Creator Parents in pure energetic form that lovingly look after us from the time we are able to individuate ourselves on earth as a separate soul, born of the divine, all the way through time until we reintegrate back in with our Creator Parent's energy, while still keeping our individuality in tact.

So...do you understand why it is a good practice to prove everything out and ask our Creator Parents to make themselves real to you here on the earth plane, and also take time to create connectivity with all living things? You see, when you can feel the loving support of the people in spirit form helping you, your Creator Parents loving and helping you, and the connection that we all have with the earth, it is at this point that you will be able to update your outdated child belief of being alone, to knowing that you never really are...ever alone! What's really awesome about updating that outdated core belief that we formed in childhood, around people always leaving us and being alone, is that once we change that belief then our Law Of Attraction changes, and we stop attracting people that leave us. Trust me when I say that it feels AMAZING to attract good people that love you and want to stay in your life.

CHAPTER 11

I Am Not Important

So now we get to the **GRANDDADDY** of all outdated childhood core beliefs. This sneaky monster belief is one that says that we are NOT important, we are over looked, no one cares about us, and we are not special or chosen, and because of this we can never get anyone's attention, and if by chance we do, we can never keep it for very long. This outdated core belief is like a choking vine that chokes out every bit of happiness that tends to crop up in our lives simply because we truly believe that we do not deserve to be happy.

This core belief in childhood is formed when a child suffers through verbal, emotional, sexual, and physical abuse. However, more often than not this strong belief is also formed by a child, even when there is no abuse growing up. Again, speaking with thousands of clients about this outdated core belief, it is the most common one that is formed and hard-set in childhood, and the hardest one to detect as problematic in our adult lives. This is because it could have been formed by just ONE time of a parent not being able to be there with a child at a crucial moment in their life, to lend their emotional support, yet for the rest of the child's life their parents loved and doted on them. On the flip-side, the outdated core belief could have been formed because the parents had to work, and couldn't be there as much for their child as they needed to be, or they spent too much time on solving their own problems and not enough time with their children, yet they still loved their children dearly and supported them dutifully.

The reason that this outdated belief is such a HUGE problem to correct and update as adults is that to do so means that we must be willing to admit that our parents made mistakes in the way they raised us. We also tend to minimize our experiences with this and convince ourselves that other children had it way worse than what we had. In this we feel that we have no right to feel rejected and overlooked in the way that we do. Also, in order to come to terms with this, for many of us, it is necessary for us to be honest with ourselves about when our parents didn't extend unconditional love to us, or give us enough time and attention.

The difficulty in this comes at us in two ways, first we tend to feel a need to fiercely defend our parents out of our own unconditional love for them. Deep in our minds we think and believe that if we love and defend our parents enough, at some point we will become important to them, they will choose us more, and in that we will receive more acceptance and unconditional love from our parents in return. Second, if we don't feel this need then we tend to blame our parents for all of our problems. The real truth in all of this is that at the end of the day, it is truly our own selves that are creating our problems from outdated core beliefs, as we reach the age of accountability.

Unfortunately, it is also our own consciousness that has convinced our brain through feelings of shame, fear, and lack of acceptance, that we are so rotten and bad at a core level that we don't really deserve to be chosen to receive any of the attention that we are craving. At this point we emotionally distance from the parts of ourselves that hurt the most, and then we turn around and give that emotional support to other people. We do this because we believe that if we give the emotional support that we didn't get as children to others around us, that we can heal our pain of emotional abandonment when people reciprocate the emotional support we are giving them back to us. Unfortunately most of the people that we give emotional support to never give it back to us. To make matters worse, even if they did it would make us feel uncomfortable because we would feel so undeserving of it, that at that point we wouldn't be able to accept it.

This is when our Law of Attraction really goes to town in kicking our butts because this outdated core childhood belief of not feeling important or worthy of emotional support shows up in every area of our lives. This is why we fall in love with people that are already in relationships, only to feel excruciating pain when the person doesn't feel the same about us. Or...the person we are attracted to starts out showing intense interest in us, only to then end up staying with their current partner, that we probably didn't know about, or even worse, they move onto someone new. Then there is the being attracted to a person that can't commit to a relationship with us and they end up cheating with someone else. And last but not least, the person that we fall deeply in love with that never gets the courage up to even speak with us, even though we feel such a strong connection with them. To make matters worse, when we finally do attract a person that wants to give us all the love, affection, and attention that we deserve, we are turned off by this behavior because we feel like we are being smothered...when in truth we really just feel that we don't deserve it, and it makes us feel uncomfortable. And the list goes on and on when it comes to personal relationships. Over the years it is this outdated core belief that has caused MOST of the relationship problems in my clients lives, and it is the MOST talked about one.

This outdated core belief of not feeling important or worthy of emotional support also shows up in our work lives. Co-workers dump work on us that isn't ours to do. We are passed over for promotions and raises. We are never given recognition for what we do. Our questions are the last to be answered. Finally, when we bring a problem to the attention of management they are minimized and often swept under the rug, and on many occasions we are blamed for the same said problems. I have spoken with many clients that will actually attract very covertly hostile work environments with this outdated childhood core belief.

This outdated core childhood belief even shows up when we are out and about running errands or having fun. This is why people cut us off in traffic. It is why people cut in front of us in line, and we accept this behavior, yet swear angrily underneath our breath. It is why waitresses and bartenders ignore us and preference other customers ahead of us. It is why we are bumped back on a flight, or in a service. Do you see where I'm going with this? If something happens and it causes a feeling inside of you to come up as not being chosen, being unimportant, overlooked, less than, or not good enough, then it is this very outdated childhood belief that is rearing it's ugly head and it would be helpful if you wouldn't ignore yourself in how you feel and ad insult to injury.

Now we get to the good part...you are the ONLY you there is... and this IS NO other like YOU! There is NO competition with you, no one that is better or worse than YOU! The truth of this matter is that you are a very loved and chosen child of two amazing, Omnipotent Creators, that are the source of everything in our infinite universes. As their child you also have inherited the same powerful energy in you that is in them, only on a smaller scale. This means that you hold space in our Universe that no one else can hold as a powerful creator in your own right.

With this said you will only feel and know your greatness, your importance, when you spend more time...well...WITH YOU! You see, in order to attract people to you that treat you with unconditional love, respect, and reciprocity, you need to first have a loving, emotionally supportive relationship with yourself. Oh...you don't know how? Think about the kindest person that you have ever known, and treat yourself they way they would treat you. Listen to yourself, take time with yourself to work through difficult emotions, allow yourself to play and feel good, reward yourself for meeting your goals and getting things done. Show up and be committed to your own well-being every day. Now do you see what I mean? You are you...and there is no other...so as Shakespeare said, "to thine own self be true!"

CHAPTER 12

Changing Our Core Beliefs

So now that we have gone through some of the major, and more common, outdated core beliefs that we bring from childhood into our adult lives, creating problems that are fairly disruptive, stressful, and painful, let's get into **how to update and change** those outdated core beliefs. The major part of changing outdated childhood core belief is being aware of what they are, AND when we are putting them into play. Most of us don't pay attention to all the thought chatter that goes on in our minds, however, we **ARE VERY** aware of when we feel negative emotions. This is when easy repetitive work comes into play, because there are four simple questions, that if you check in with yourself 3-4 times a day to get the answers, you will change your life tremendously in as little as 15-30 days!

Why you ask?

Simply because it is scientifically proven that if you do something new repetitively 30 times, this in turn will scratch a new groove in your brain, and **WAHLAH**...you have just formed a new habit! If you do that new activity over 2,000 times, then it will become an automatic reflex.

Now, on to the four questions that will change your life if you are acting on them to get the answers:

1. **What are you feeling?** No, I don't mean like you feel like crying or you feel angry, you feel happy or excited...what are you REALLY feeling according to your beliefs? Are you feeling like no once cares? Are you feeling left out, unimportant, or like you are always losing at life? Are you feeling alone or lonely? Are you feeling like people talk bad about you and don't like you? Or...are you feeling like everything is somehow always working out for you. Are you feeling that if you just give yourself enough time to figure something out that you will always do better this time, or next time? Are you feeling happy with what you are doing in life? Are you feeling like people are choosing you, loving you, and accepting you? This is what I mean when the question is asked...how am I feeling?

2. **What are you doing about HOW you are feeling?** With this question you want to take time to be aware of how you are handling how you feel, and what your thoughts are about how you feel. Are you beating yourself up for making a mistake in your head, while you are feeling rejected and abandoned, or are you taking your time to close your eyes for a few minutes to talk yourself kindly through this feeling? Are you trying to ignore your feeling of fear and anxiety around a certain situations, telling yourself to stop being such a coward, or are you showing up for yourself to understand why you're afraid, and gently talking yourself through the fear? Do you see why the second question is so important? It is because if you are lovingly parenting your inner child self through whatever

feeling it is that you are having then you will have an much easier time working through that feeling. When you do this you begin to both understand, trust, BELIEVE, and feel that your adult self can handle the situation at hand.

3. **What is the core belief driving the feeling?** Again, it would be helpful to dig deep to get to the real core belief. Do you believe that you always have to see the worst case scenario so that you can prepare for anything that could go wrong? Do you believe that people will always leave you, especially the ones you really love, and that you are always alone? Do you believe that you do not deserve to have good things in your life? Do you believe that money is bad and there is never enough of it for you? And this list goes on...and on. Or...do you believe the opposite of all of this? It would be helpful to be brutally honest with yourself because as much as it hurts when someone lies to you...it hurts even worse when you lie to yourself!

4. **How can you change your outdated childhood core belief to drive better feelings more of the time?** If the feeling is good...DON'T CHANGE IT...do more to positively reinforce and perpetuate the feeling! If you are experiencing a negative feeling then ask yourself how you can update and change that core belief to where it will drive more good feelings, based on the fact that you are older now, you have more life experience to pull from now, and because of this you are much better at creating what you truly need and want now.

For example, if your core belief is one that says that you are ugly, unimportant, overlooked, unaccepted, and shunned by people, then change it to simply say…I am beautiful and/or amazing, I am chosen, and I am loved. You can say this honestly because you are choosing yourself, because you truly believe that you are beautiful and amazing, and you are loving both yourself and the life that you are gifted with by your Creator Parents. If you believe that you are alone or abandoned then change that core belief to simply say…there is no loss or separation, there is only learning more, doing more, and being more. If you believe that you are always wrong and bad to your souls core then you can change that belief to simply say…there is no bad or good there is only negative and positive polarity, and in that there is only learning, doing more, and being more with no judgment. Do you see how simple this is?

After you have memorized these for questions, then put sticky notes all around your house and work space, where your eyes constantly look with the first lead in question…"how do I feel?" If it's a sticky note at work and you need to be more cryptic the just write…"-feel?" From there practice asking these questions, and giving yourself honest answers, in the morning, at noon, after supper, and right before bedtime.

You will find that self-awareness is the key that unlocks the door to a whole world of happiness that you have never known before. In all honesty though, in order for you to get to that big, warm, safe, love-filled living room, you must walk down a bit of a dark hall of negative childhood memories in order to get there. It may seem a bit scary at first, however, if you will just remember that you have lots of very loving, very BIG benevolent beings, including your adult self walking you down that dark hallway, then this part of you changing outdated childhood core beliefs is really not difficult at all.

Whenever it would seem like I was in a dark place in my life, I would close my eyes and remember all the times I made it through difficult times. I would also remember how I was able to solve whatever problem that I faced, and how I had been protected through the whole ordeal. From there I would breath deeply, turn on my inner light of trust, and invoke the Universal Law of Faith. After that the dark place that I was in would lift and dissipate like a fog, along with any worry, stress, anxiety, or fear that I felt. You can do this, too, if you practice it enough, and it only takes a few minutes to do this. Oh... and I promise that you will feel much better afterwards.

CHAPTER 13

Creating Daily Affirmations

Ok, so here is where the second part of changing outdated core beliefs is implemented. This is a simple step that only takes a few seconds at a time to do once you get it all set up. You see in order to change a core belief you have to take small, easy, repetitive steps to reprogram you subconscious brain. Some people think that this is a long, arduous task, however, nothing could be further from the truth.

With this said the first simple repetitive step to take is to create daily affirmations. Below are some affirmations that have worked for me very well:

1. There is no loss or separation, there is only learning, doing more, and being more.

2. Everything always works our for me.

3. I am beautiful/handsome, chosen, and loved.

4. I am wealthy and abundance in all things.

5. Money comes to me easily and in large amounts.

6. I know how to spend and invest money wisely and I enjoy doing so.

7. I am intelligent and gifted and I love learning new things.

8. I am really good at solving problems.

9. I can easily manifest anything I put my mind, heart, and soul to.

10. I am trustworthy therefore I can trust.

11. I love my life and my life loves me back.

12. The Universe and God loves me and desires to help me.

13. I enjoy exercising and shaping my body the way I want it to be.

14. I enjoy finding truth and making good memories in every day.

15. I am safe and I love exploring new places and things.

Do you get what I mean in making up simple, positive affirmations? You can use the ones above or make up ones of your own. That it completely up to you, however once you are done then either write them on sticky notes or put them in framed messages all over your home and workplace in places where they will catch your gaze most of the time. Once this is done, every time you see and affirmation say it out loud or under your breath at least three times.

Now I'm going to tell you WHY this is so effective in changing your outdated childhood core beliefs. Your brain is nothing but a quantum computer, embedded in human flesh, and attached to a human soul. All computers need to be "programmed" in order to do whatever task you want them to do...right? Well, your brain is no different in that if you want to feel better emotions, more of the time, you have to program your brain with more positive beliefs instead of the fear-based ones that were taught to you as a child.

Now we get to the good part. Ninety percent of what a human looks at while they are awake, is what generates emotions (energy-in-motion), which in turn ends up forming into a belief if looked at enough. Ten percent of what a human listens to ends up reinforcing the emotion that was generated by what a human sees, or looks at. That is why pictures speak louder than hearing words, and when you combine the two of them, then the emotion that is generated is so strong that a person ends up creating what they are looking at and hearing. This is why they call television shows, "programming," because it's teaching your brain to think and act in a certain way.

If you want to take the above activity to a more intense and faster level, take pictures of times when you are creating awesome memories. From there put the affirmations into the pictures, and hang them everywhere that your eyes gaze most often in a day. Now what you are doing is proving to your brain with a good memories that these affirmations are true. This goes a long way in convincing your soul that you really have grown and learned more in your life on earth, and that things are actually much better than what your brain is telling you.

If you want to double the power and speed of not having so many major, catastrophic problems, then combine doing the above, with reading 10 pages a day of positive self-help books, and/or entrepreneurial books like, "The Prosperity Bible," every day. I love writing this part of the book because these simple and easy steps and activities involves you being able to get creative!

CHAPTER 14

Sleep Subconscious Reprogramming

Ok, now that we have gotten to the conscious, awake part of the mind, it's time to get to the subconscious part of the mind. So here's what's really strange about our brains. So you think that when you go to sleep that your brain shuts off and stops taking in information while you sleep...right? Well, I hate to tell you this but...it doesn't! Your subconscious brain takes in and processes information 24/7.

Now that you have this information let's go a bit deeper. The conscious mind, or awake part of the brain, is the creative mind. The subconscious part of the brain is the mind of habit. This is the part of the brain where we are using all of the core beliefs that were hard set in our brain by the time we were seven years old. When we are awake we spend around 5% of our time operating from our conscious creative mind, and 95% of the time we are operating out of our subconscious mind...the mind of habit and outdated childhood core beliefs. What's even more interesting is that in our awake hours we only have a 10% impact on changing our subconscious mind's core beliefs.

So how do we really get into effectively changing the subconscious brain faster and more efficiently...right? Once again I have a simple solution that is easy to implement. First take all of the positive affirmations that you want your outdated core beliefs to turn into, that you have already written down in the previous chapter, and write them all down on one sheet of paper. Now write down what your perfect life would look like today, right as you are reading this.

Details I tell ya...**it's ALL in the details**. When you are writing out your life story of what your perfect life looks like, go into EXTREME detail! From the amount of money that you have in the bank right now (*hint...dream big or go home), to how much you make in a given month. How do you make money in your perfect life...through investing, passive income, through a business you love...how? What types of vehicles do you drive...from the color...to the make and model...to the year...what do you zoom zoom around in? What type(s) of house(s) do you own? Who are your friends and neighbors? How have you changed your body...have you gained or lost weight? Have you had cosmetic surgery? How have you changed your personality to be the person you truly want to be? Who is your mate...what do they look like? Any children or no? Who is your mentor...do you have a mentor? Who are your perfect customers and clients? GET SPECIFIC AND DETAILED in your life story, ok. Oh...and when you write everything down, make sure you write it so that it is easy for you to read.

Now that you have that part done, take out your cellphone and while playing soft music that you like in the background, record yourself reading your affirmations first, and then go into reading your "perfect life story," with all the joy and excitement as if you were already in the middle of living it. If you find it difficult to imagine your perfect life with joy then read all of the above while making sure that a smile is on your face the whole time. This is usually is a lot easier for people who aren't good at acting or pretending.

Now that you have recorded that video on your cellphone, every night before you go to bed, while your cellphone is charging, put the video that you made of your perfect life story in a replay loop, and play it all night while you are sleeping. You see, your subconscious mind doesn't know that it's listening to a recording of you, and because of this it really thinks that it is you talking with it. This in turn makes your brain really believe what it hears in the repetitive speaking of your positive affirmations and perfect life story. Because your subconscious brain keeps hearing this recording in your voice, and it deduces that it hasn't made all the things it hears come true yet, it sets about making what it hears all of the time at night happen in real life. You see, by doing this you are setting your subconscious mind into automatic problem solving mode 24/7. Make sure to play this recording every night softly in the background as you sleep, and you will find that so many of your goals will be met or exceeded to the extent that you have to update your perfect life story every three to six months.

I have found that when I combined all three things:

1. Affirmations every where I looked.

2. Reading 10 pages of self-help/entrepreneurial books a day.

3. Playing my subconscious "Perfect Life" recording on my cell-phone every night while I slept.

Something AMAZING happened! I broke through the ceiling of only making 3-10k a month for 7 years. It was after I starting doing all three of these things to change my outdated childhood core beliefs that my problems seemed to disappear and my income soared to around 20k per month and it is still going up to this day!

However...even with these simple steps...I took it things even further, because I had picked up a bad habit of smoking cigarettes to relieve the stress of a divorce, children that struggled with drug addiction, and the death of one of my own children, and I wanted to kick that bad habit to the curb. Not to mention, in the middle of this all, time seemed to march on like the energizer bunny and I found myself slipping into per-menopause (I started getting old), and my weight gain was becoming unbearable, so I figured that I could lose weight while I was at it, too.

And you know what?

I have taken this simple and powerful method of problem solving even further!

Because the first part of problem solving had been so simple and easy to put into play for me, I decided to ramp it up with other simple and awesome manifesting techniques. If you bear with me just a wee bit longer...I will tell you those pivotal secrets now.

CHAPTER 15

Don't Look At What You Don't Want!

I know...I know...life tends to be like a bad wreck that you can't stop looking at as you drive by...right? I mean every time you turn on the news all you hear is one bad news story after another and all you can think about is how this world is going to hell in a hand basket! So not wanting to hear a bunch of bad news you get on your computer to see what your friends are doing and before you know it you find yourself sucked into other peoples drama. **SHEESH!**

So here is an easy bit of information to remember. A human creates 90% of what they see with their eyes. This means that if you are constantly looking at bad events in the news, you will constantly feel fear and disgust. This in turn will influence you to subconsciously go into helping the larger collective of people around you into creating similar events around you in your local area.

Another thing that we do is constantly look at our bills and the money that we DON'T have in our bank account. When we do this we create more bills, and even less money. Finally, we tend to be drawn into constantly watching negative personal interactions between people that we know, or we obsess about looking at someone that we want, who is currently not paying any attention to us. This in turn creates more negativity in the people around us, or more of the person that we want ignoring us.

With this said, what I have learned about manifesting and getting what I want, instead of having to solve problems all of the time, is that the most powerful way to create what I want is to:

STOP LOOKING AT WHAT I DON'T WANT!

The minute I hid my bills and refused to look at them until I had the money to pay on them, the less more bills came to me. The minute I stopped looking at my bank account when I was low on money and only looked at money that I had coming in, I was able to create greater amounts of money. The minute I stopped waiting for and worrying that clients weren't setting calls, and started doing something else that was productive, creative, and fun, was when my clients started booking calls. Oh...and get this...the minute I refused to watch it snow, closed my curtains and only allowed myself to watch good weather video's, was when it would stop snowing. Haha....in doing this I caused a whole winter storm to go around me in a 25 mile radius.

If you find that the person you are wanting and obsessing over is ghosting or bread-crumbing you, STOP WATCHING THEM ON SOCIAL MEDIA!!! First of all, nothing you see on social media is going to be accurately true simply because people use social media to make them LOOK GOOD...not to be brutally honest about their lives. Second, when you keep looking at the person that is ghosting you online, they can actually feel your energetic pull and it makes them believe, that because you are focused on them, they can take all the time they need or want in getting ready to give you attention. If you find that you don't have the personal discipline to stop watching certain people on social media, unfriend or unfollow them until you do, ok. Oh sure, you might offend a few people, however, it would be helpful to remember that you are NOT responsible for other people's emotional reactions. You are **only** responsible for YOU, YOUR LIFE, and WHAT YOU ARE CREATING IN YOUR LIFE & WORLD, ok.

I remember when I went into writing my first two books, back to back, I had so many marketing friends blowing up my inbox and feed, even after I had stated that I needed time to focus on writing my books, that I had to unfriend and unfollow most of them in order to curb my tendency to get sucked into the social media time waste vortex. When I got done writing my two books most all of those friends came back, simply because they understood what I was doing and why I was doing it. To this day those same friends follow me and look to me now as a business leader and problem solver because I not only know how to keep my focus on what I want, I also know how to keep strong boundaries and not get distracted into looking at what I don't want.

On that note, it you want to create less problems and more of what you DO want, it would be helpful to STOP WATCHING MAIN STREAM MEDIA NEWS! I am not saying this from any political bias at all. I am saying this because it was only when I stopped watching main stream media news, and television all together, that my income started to sky-rocket, I didn't have so many problems, because I wasn't so worried all of the time, and I began to relax and enjoy life a lot more. Now I watch videos to learn new things that interest me, I watch documentaries, and I spend more time interacting with my loved ones, my dog, and the beautiful outside world in nature.

Now I will tell you the other secret behind not looking at what you don't want. It's not just that you create what you look at the most through the Universal Law Of Attraction, you also create more of what you want with less problems by using the Universal Law Of Energy. The Universal Law Of Energy is when you pull your conscious focus away from something, after putting the desire for it out into the Universal Energetic Field, you pull it to you at a time that is perfect for you and everyone involved in you having what you want. Using the Universal Law of Energy is putting perfect time into play in your life, and when you can trust yourself, AND Universal Timing...awe hell...you're gonna warp speed ahead in life like nobodies business!!!

If you think about it, have you ever wondered why psychopaths and sociopaths have such power over average humans? It is because whatever they think of in their mind is the truth and they live by it, without fear, in order to win at all costs. They do not live in the reality that the rest of humanity lives in, and they do not feel the emotions that average humans feel, they fake it. In this they only look at what they want, and they refuse to look at or accept any other reality outside of this. This is why so many serial killers go such long in time before they are caught. This doesn't mean that you should become a serial killer to get what you want, however, it does show you what you should be focused on in order to create exactly what you want! To be fair, this is also what Olympic gold medalists, and professional athletes practice in order to be the best in whatever they do.

It is good to remain singularly focused on one thing at a time, until you are able to manifest whatever you want with it. When you practice this you need less information in order create just one thing, instead of multiple things. This means that with less information needed, there are fewer problems because it is easier to gain access to the lesser amount of information needed. My high school Spanish teacher taught me the most valuable lesson I ever learned in school, and that was to keep things simple, and knock out my tasks one at time. To this day I take things...one moment...one feeling...one core belief...one day at a time. This is the main reason why I have very few problems, more peace, and the ability to feel more joy in my life.

CHAPTER 16

Set Gratefulness As A Baseline

Have you ever wondered why happy people are so happy? It is because they are so grateful for what they have in their lives! Well...I'm really not the "Polly-Anna" type of person, simply because I have a tendency to be a more logical thinker, however, I have learned from actual experience that gratefulness has a tendency to attract more wealth, and less problems.

One time I had a flat tire and I lived two miles up, on top of a mountain. Normally a flat tire was not a problem for me because I have changed many a tire in my day. However, this day was different because as I set about changing my flat tire, I noticed that all of my tire jacks were not tall enough for my four wheel drive. My nearest neighbors were all the way down at the base of the mountain, and I didn't want to hike all the way down there to get help. To put it bluntly, I had a real problem because my truck was my life-line to basic supplies that I needed to survive on the mountain, and now I couldn't go to town to get what I needed.

After trying everything I knew to get my truck high enough off the ground to change the tire I sat down and just took time to cry out my frustration. My outdated core belief that I was working on changing at that time, was one that said that I was not good enough for things to go smoothly for me, so unexpected bad things were always happening to me. It also hurt to know that when I needed help, there was no one near enough to help me.

After I cleared all the negative emotion away with tears, I set about doing things around my cabin to get ready for a hike down the mountain the next day, and I gently told myself that everything always worked out for me, because my Creator Parents loved me so much and wanted me to have a life of ease. From there I started to be grateful for everything that I had, that brought a smile to my face and made my life good.

It wasn't long before I felt better, and a couple of hours later as I sat on my front porch petting my dog, my neighbors from the base of the mountain drove up. They had some food that they thought I might like, so they decided to drop it off for me. When they saw that I had a flat tire the husband immediately set about helping me change it with the right jack that they had with them, and soon I was on my way to town for much needed supplies. Boy howdy was I ever happy, and even more grateful, for the caring neighbors that I had been blessed with!

What this confirmed in my brain was that the outdated child-hood core beliefs of not being important, loved or cared about, being a bad person, and that because of this life had to be filled with unexpected hardships, was totally false and untrue now. Now the new core beliefs that I was busy reprogramming my brain with began to ring true. I really was beautiful, chosen, important, and loved. Life really could be lived with ease and in peace, and everything always really did work out for me.

Well after that the good fortune just kept coming as I did more business that day, after I got back home, than I had done in a long time. I found that this felt so good that I made it a habit to write down what I was grateful for every morning before I got into the work part of my day. What this did for me was reinforce the new, more positive core beliefs that I was reprogramming my mind with AND it also helped me to attract more of whatever I needed, and also money, without all the worry and struggle. Now what I would deem as instant fixes to my problems, or "miracles" as I call them, have begun to happen more often, especially when it came to flat tires.

Since that time on the mountain, there have been at least three other times of having flat tires where "miracles" have happened for me, not to mention all the other help that I received in the five years I spent on top of my mountain. It only took about a month before I had formed a new habit of being constantly grateful. I was also able to really feel how good it felt when everything always did start working out for me in a good way!

What's interesting about setting a habit of being constantly grateful is that it hooks in so nicely to the genuine feeling of happiness and joy that I can feel more often now. I smile more, and people like to be around me more. My dog wags her tail more and wants to snuggle with me more, and my clients are a lot nicer to me now. Most of all I am feeling more connected, accepted, and loved now...simply because I am grateful for both the big, medium, and small things in my life now.

You see, the secret to setting gratefulness as a baseline and foundation for changing outdated core childhood beliefs, is that it gives us PROOF that our new positive core belief is right. From there you are then able to pass that information on to your brain. In return your brain forms and feels a positive emotion for all the positive things that you are creating. If there is one pivotal action that has changed both my outdated core beliefs, and my life in general, it has been taking time to set a habit of being grateful in all things.

CHAPTER 17

Let It Flow & Ride The Waves

Believe it or not, problem solving is a lot like surfing. It's all about riding waves of emotions until they dissipate, and then once they are cleared out of your energetic field of focus, you can get down to gathering all of the information that you need in which to solve your problem.

So many times instead of allowing our emotions to flow out of us, we repress them, swallow them, or shove them deep down inside of us, especially if they are considered to be negative emotions. When we do this our emotions (energy-in-motion) is stored in the muscles in our bodies and because most of those stored emotions are negative in nature, after longer periods of time this begins to cause imbalances in our physical bodies, that surface in the forms of diseases and injuries. The more we repress our emotions, the more disease and injuries we end up experiencing in our physical bodies. This is why when you get massages, facials, acupuncture, or any type of body work done, afterwards you will find that you tend to be very emotional. This is because all the emotion in your muscles have been moved into your bodies energetic flow as if you are experiencing them fresh, all over again.

We repress our emotions for several reasons. The number one reason is through generational beliefs and soul injuries handed down to us from our parents and generations up from them. One of those major generational beliefs that is usually taught and handed down through multiple generations is that children should be seen and not heard. Children often are considered to be ignorant, rash, and without reason, so it is believed that they should be quiet and willing to listen and learn most of the time. Nothing could be further from the truth.

Children are actually born in their purest state of energy when they are young in their minds and bodies, and they are actually great sources of deep truth and knowledge. Many children have actually lived many lives, and it is while they are very young that they can still remember what it is like to live in the spirit world, from where they have just come. They also have the ability to remember a lot of things from previous lifetimes occurring before the one in which they are currently in. Children also have a heightened sense of extra-sensory perception, and for the first six months of a babies life they can still see and hear higher level spirits, close to our Creator Parents, singing to them and talking with them. There are times when a baby cries in a deeply saddened or grieving way and this is because as they grow older they can no longer hear the "Angels" sing, and they begin to feel alone. You can tell when a baby is actually seeing someone in that is near them in their spirit body, because the baby will look right past you at something very intently, and as you turn to see what they are looking at, there is seemingly nothing there outside of a bedroom wall. There are also many times that a child's make believe playmate will actually be their Spirit Guide, or an earthbound spirit (ghost).

Another generational belief that is handed down to children is that crying is an action of rebellion that should be stopped at any cost including using physical violence and/or harm to stop it. Remember when we as children would cry and our parents would tell us that if we didn't stop, they would give us something to cry about? The simple truth about this is that a child's cry is how children get their parents attention.

After parenting three children I learned to understand what the different cries meant. Some cries meant that my children needed something, some cries meant that they were hurting physically, some cries meant that they were angry, and still some cries from my children held a deep vibration of sadness and grief. As children grow older crying is combined with language, again, to enhance what they are saying so that they can get their parents attention. It is a form of communication filled with raw emotion. Sometimes it can be done out of rebellion, however, most of the time it is done with the child is feeling intense emotions.

There are several reasons why a lot of parents go out of their way to stop a child's cry. First of all the parents wants to help the child with whatever it is crying for and needs. Second, sometimes the child's cry is irritating the parent, some to the point of physical discomfort, and the parent wants the child to stop irritating them. Third, sometimes when a child cries the parents feel embarrassment or shame for feeling like they are not parenting the child right, so they do whatever it takes to get the child to stop crying.

Where we as humans learn that showing emotions is bad is in the plethora of ways that parents use negative ways to force their children to stop feeling their emotions. Some parents use physical aggression like spanking, citing traditions handed down through their generations that state, "if you spare the rod, you spoil the child." Other parents use isolation (time-out or standing in the corner). Some parents are more subtle and they use guilt and shame to get their children to stop feeling their emotions, while yet others use bribery. At the end of the day though, usually most children are taught to feel ashamed of experiencing negative emotions, and when we get to be adults showing that we experiencing negative emotions in public is usually taboo.

Even when children are happy, or experiencing positive emotions, if they are too loud or rambunctious, they are told to calm down and be quiet. This happens when parents are prone to being afraid of other people judging them as being bad parents, because they cannot control their own children. This in turn results in children that learn to repress and subdue their emotional energy, which results in a plethora of problems later on as the child grows into adolescence, and then adulthood.

I think the most injurious way that we learn to repress our emotions is through different societal pressures to be "normal." We must conform to what it deems as, "normal," or be left outside of societal acceptance and protection. For instance, the majority of people in our society attributes crying and sad emotions to feminine energy, and because of this, society highly influences us to think that it is not acceptable for male children to show the emotions of grieving, sadness, or crying. If male children past a certain age show these types of emotion, they are told to stop, "man-up," and if they don't stop publicly experiencing their sad emotions, people will look at them as being "weak," or being a "sissy" (feminine). However, at the same time, is is more acceptable in our society when male children feel or experience anger and aggression in public. I mean after all, "boys will be boy...right?" Society seems to encourage aggression in male children in order to mold them into being better protectors for their female mates. With this said on the other hand, currently in our society, it is ok for female children to experience sad emotions in public, however on the other hand, it is frowned upon when female children show anger or aggressive emotions in public. This is because we are not supposed to fight against a man's ability to protect us, even when that same male strength is turned against us in a way where we are being harmed. I have seen parents that actually punish their female children harshly for standing up to, and fighting, male children who are being bullies, with the school system supporting this perspective. Hell, even in all the abuse I grew up with, this view up females being, "submissive," was taught to me with severe punishment if I showed anger or aggression in any way!

As a society that is supposed to be more advanced we still have this one error in thinking and parenting, that human emotions should be divided into accepted norms for males and females and anything outside of this is not acceptable. At the end of the day though...the truth is...having ALL emotions, both positive and negative ones, is what being HUMAN is. It is how ALL humans create...with energy-in-motion (emotions). In this societal programming, our children tend to be handicapped in their ability to create in a more balanced way, simply because they are not allowed to feel a humans full array of both negative and positive emotions.

Most of our problems come from a combination of outdated childhood core beliefs, and an inability to experience and release our negative emotions without projecting them at other people. With this being said our primary goal in our adult should be to teach ourselves how to be willing and open to experiencing our own emotions, **WITHOUT PROJECTING THEM AT OTHER PEOPLE** if they are negative. The reason for this is because we cannot create at our greatest capacity if we do not allow our own "energy-in-motion" (emotions) to flow properly through us. When our energetic flow of emotions is dammed up it creates problems that overflow that dam. Well...let's be honest...we are here to SOLVE your problem not make more of them...right?

The problem with teaching ourselves in our adult lives to once again feel and release our emotions is that if we have dammed them up for years...well hells bells...we tend to get mighty scared of too much emotion coming up at one time...right? I mean what if we get too angry or sad and people don't like it and we end up looking crazy? What if we look weak when we show our emotions and people take advantage of us? What if we end up looking like an emotional wreck and like we can't handle our problems? What if we get so angry or sad that it causes a heart attack in us and we die? And...the list of fears go on and on...sigh.

I remember back to when I was around eighteen years old that I had repressed so much fear, rage, and grief down in my soul, that I began to have irregular heart beats. My heart rate was unusually high all of the time, and I would have times when my heart would be so fast that I would get light headed and think I was going to die. This continued until I made the commitment to heal my soul, and in that I had to teach myself to cry again.

For years I never allowed myself to cry because in being abused, if I cried, it showed my abusers that I was weak...and I hated myself for showing weakness and crying. When I first began to reteach myself to cry, at the age of thirty-two, I first had to overcome the fear that if I cried that I would feel too much emotion at one time and die. I had to do the same thing with feeling rage and anger. Because I was severely punished if I showed any anger as a child, I had to teach myself as an adult that it was ok to be angry, only if I remembered to not project it at any other living thing.

The more I faced my fear of feeling negative emotions and allowed myself to feel them, the more I healed in my soul, and with that my problems began to melt away. I also started to have less and less irregular heart rhythms. What I learned from this was that my soul would not allow more emotion to surface than my physical body could handle. To this day though I still don't have the capacity to cry as much as normal people, who haven't been through the abuse I went through, are able to do. I also still have to be very aware of when I feel the tremble of the emotion of rage coming up and make sure to not project it in any way that would hurt another living being. This is because the amount of repressed anger from past abuse is much greater in me than most people who haven't had the experiences that I have. I guess what I am trying to say is there is no wrong or right amount of emotions that should be felt. Some people can cry more than others, while some people are setting on way more rage and anger than other and have to be more cautious when that emotion comes up. Emotional energy is different and specific to every individual human, therefore it would be helpful to not judge yourself for having more or less than another person, ok.

With that said, why did my problems begin to melt away when I was able to feel and release negative emotions, you ask?

The reason for this was when I encountered a problem I allowed myself to take time to release any negative emotion I had around it. When I did this first thing, right away, my problem was then downgraded to being more of an information gathering mission so that I could get past a block that I had encountered. Without the outdated childhood core belief and the negative emotion in the way, clouding my ability to find a solution to getting around any given block, I was able to access and/or find the information that I needed to get around any said block in a much easier, more rapid, and peaceful way.

This is why this chapter is called, let it flow and ride the waves. This is why solving problems is a lot like surfing. Think of emotions as water, another energetic form that you can tangibly sense with all five senses. If you don't dam those negative emotions up and you allow them to flow like water, it is at this point that you are less likely to drown in them, or get bogged down by them for long periods of time. You see when you allow emotions to flow through you, as they are designed to do, then you can paddle through the negative ones until you get enough information to get to a wave of good emotions, and upon launching into the wave of good emotional energy, you can ride it in a creative way until it comes to an end. From there you rest in the baseline of gratefulness until another swell of negative emotion comes, or if your lucky...you just get ready to ride another massive wave of good emotions. You will find that when you do this that the only problem you have to focus on is just making sure you have enough information to stay and/or steer away from any rock outcroppings!

CHAPTER 18

Self-Talk

How many times have you caught yourself thinking that you were stupid for doing something that didn't turn out so well, while verbally chewing yourself out for not doing something different? I can honestly say I used to do it way more than I should have. That was when I was at the height of problems cropping up on a regular basis, disrupting my life in dramatic ways. I can honestly say that my life at that time was one big drama that nobody wanted to hear about, after they listened to me complain about it for the first five minutes. You see, when you talk negatively about yourself...to yourself...you are reinforcing outdated childhood core beliefs, lowering your energetic levels, and turning people around you off, all at the same time.

Think back to when you would have to listen to your parents lecture you on how bad your mistakes were, exactly what you did that what wrong, and how bad you were for making the mistake? Did that ever happen to you? Guess what...if it happened once...it happened a lot! You see, it is very rare to experience a chewing out like this as a child just once, unless your parents for the most part practiced positive reinforcement, and you did something to really frightened them. Most of the time parents lecture children in a negative way, it is because this is how they were parented, and they have already formed a core belief and habit of doing this with their own children.

So for this next part let's go over some basics. The way humans create in simple terms goes like this, we think about what we want, then we talk about it, which in turn creates a good feeling about having it, which in turns brings that "whatever we want" into our physical world. Now here is another simple truth. When you do, see, or hear something thirty times, you create a new groove in your brain which creates what we call a "habit." A habit is when we begin to do things in repetition without giving it much thought.

I gave you those truths because when a child hears adults they love and respect chewing them out and/or talking negatively about what they do, what they are going to do, how they are behaving, or who they are...after only thirty times of hearing this type of talk...the child at that point forms not only a negative core belief about themselves, that also form a habit of thinking about and perceiving themselves in a negative way. Not only that, the child also forms a habit of talking in this same negative way to themselves. I know this because this is what I did for almost forty-two years of my life.

It was only when I began to close my eyes, picture myself as a young child, and begin to practice talking with myself in the compassionate, nurturing way that I never heard my parents speak in, that my problems began to lessen, and my view of myself was not so dismal...and believe me when I say that I didn't see myself in a good light at all. I thought I was fat, stupid, bad, and a horrible parent that couldn't get it right, even though I loved my kids more than life itself!

This is why I had to begin by seeing myself as a child before I could speak with myself in a kind and gentle way.

After I was able to form a habit of speaking with myself in a much kinder, compassionate, and gentle way, being the parent to myself that I never had, I was able to talk myself through some of the toughest problems I could have ever imagined with ease. After I formed a habit of talking myself through major life changing problems, having built up more trust in myself, my problems began to lessen. From there, because I had more confidence and trust in myself, my Creator Parents, and the Universe, I began to change and update my outdated childhood core beliefs. Problems for me now are at an all time low. Now it feels great to stay more in creative, positive flow energy most of the time.

Do things still happen that catch me off guard?

Yes!

Does it hurt sometimes...like the death of my Son?

You BETCHA!

Is it a problem?

No!

Why?

Because, I know how to let my emotions flow in one end of me, and out the other end, without trying to stop them, or repress them. Because, I know how to get the information I need to solve things that seem problematic in an easy and logical way. Because I have set good habits of being grateful all of the time, and speaking with myself in a much more positive way. Because I have formed a habit of only focusing on what I do want and not on what I don't want. And finally, because in my reality now I am committed to showing up in an emotionally supportive way for myself each and every day, and this means that there are really no problems, there are only questions and SOLUTIONS that I enjoy finding!

CHAPTER 19

Solving Your Problem

Now that you have all the information on HOW to solve your problem, let's go through a run-down on solving an actual problem. This is so that you can see the problem solving mentality at work, ok. With this said let's stick with the problem we have been talking about throughout this entire book. By the way, this is a problem that actually happened to me about four years ago. I know this may not be your particular problem, however, you can use the same easy process to get through your problem and to the answer swiftly and painlessly, if you follow the example.

So...I'm going down the road on holiday to visit my Son, and I have around $250 in the bank for the trip there and back. Out of nowhere I hear a loud thumping sound, so I pull of at the next exit about 1000ft down the road. By then there is steam coming out from under the hood of my truck, and my engine light goes on, so I quickly turn my truck off and go to look under the hood. There is antifreeze spewing every where, the fan is all chewed up, and I know that I cannot drive any further down the road.

I get back into the truck, close my eyes, breath deeply and clear my head for about five minutes. From there I think about all the things I am grateful for. I am grateful for no getting into a wreck on the highway with a broke down truck. I am grateful for the money that I do have in my bank account. I am grateful that my cell-phone works. I am grateful that I am safe, and so on and so forth. Once I am calm and feeling better in what I am grateful for then I close my eyes again and ask my Creator Parents to help me get through the situation that I am currently in with peace and ease, and again, I am grateful that I can ask for help and know that it will be given.

Once that is done I picture myself as a child and I speak with myself in a kind and reassuring way. I tell myself, "Dawn Maree, you didn't know this was going to happen, you didn't do anything wrong, and you are not a bad person. In fact, you are a truly loving and kind person that want's to see Chris and love on him, and because of this we will be sure to make a way for this to happen. We have solved problems before so we know we can do it again and we will this time, too. Our Creator Parents love us so very much and they are helping us, and because of this everything really does always work out for us, ok. So with this said, chin up and let's get things done so that we can go see Chris, ok." Now that I have spoken to myself in a kind and concise way it is now time for me to engage my brain and begin to act.

I don't have enough money to get my truck fixed, but fortunately I do have insurance to pay for it to be towed. I also have enough money to pay for a cab to take me the rest of the way to my Son's house. On the way to my destination I find more to be grateful for, like the fact that I work from home, in an online business, and I get paid on a daily basis. I am grateful that my Son has an extra room that I can work out of, and I am grateful that the tow truck driver, and the cab driver are so nice.

When I arrive at my destination my Son is so excited to see me that any concerns about the problem I was having melt away immediately. We visit, go out, have a good time, and make tons of good memories. Everyday before he wakes up, I am able to work and make more money and in no time at all my bank account starts to look better. We end up having one of the most memorable weekends I have ever had with my Son to date. Even though I have more money by the time Monday rolls around, I still don't have enough money to get my truck fixed, but I do remember that I just bought the truck a few weeks ago, so I call the dealer to ask if they can help. Not wanting to lose a good customer, the dealer agrees to come and pick both the truck and myself up, bring me back to my home, and fix the truck at no cost to me. The only draw back is that I have to wait for them to find a reason to be in the area that my Son lives in, like picking up cars at auctions nearby.

Not liking being away from home, once again I breath deeply, close my eyes, and bring myself to a calm place again. This time, and I picture my child self squirming around and wanting to be home already, so the self talk is a bit different. I start of by saying, "Dawn Maree I know your uncomfortable child but I promise you that this won't last forever, and besides, we might not be able to see Chris for a long time after this. With this said let's do everything we can to love Chris, give him lots of great Mommy memories, and save up as much money as we can so that when we get home we can do fun things on our own, ok." Boy howdy did my child self love to hear this!

After this self-talk, my Son and his partner agreed to let me stay however long I needed, until I could get back home. True to my word, I worked in the spare bedroom in the mornings, cooked for my Son and his partner throughout the day, made sure to help clean the apartment, and spent time making as many good memories with my Son as I possibly could. Sometimes we would go for walks, sometimes we would just watch TV shows together, and sometimes we would go out to eat, or go out to his favorite place for coffee. Regardless, it was the first time in six years that I had ever been able to spend quality time with him and the next two weeks flew by so fast! By the end of two weeks the dealer was ready to come and get both my truck and myself, and my Son was grateful that I had been able to stay longer than I ever had since he lived in that apartment. With that said, I can't tell you how good it felt to be back home on my mountain, with my truck in the shop being fixed...at NO COST to me.

Well...I wasn't quite out of the woods yet. I still lived 2 miles up on top of a mountain, and I had no way to get to town to get any supplies that I needed to survive daily life. Once again I began to be grateful that this happened in the late fall before the snow fell, and it was easy to get access to my remote cabin. I was also very grateful for a neighbor at the bottom of the mountain that was always checking on me to make sure that I was ok. I was feeling so grateful that everything had worked out for me so well so far, that right as I was in that state of gratefulness, just as I was setting out to hike down the mountain to hitch-hike my way to the nearest town eleven miles away, that same neighbor called to ask if I needed anything. WHELP...as a matter of fact...I sighed deeply with relief...as I told him what had happened and that I needed a ride to town for food and supplies. And...once again...it felt so good to be able to have help come to me just in the nick of time because now I could REALLY feel AND believe my new core belief that everything really did all work out for me! A week later I had my truck back working better than ever, tons of amazing new memories with my Son, and an unfailing trust in myself and my Creator Parents, that I could solve any and all problems or blocks that I ran into with not only peace, but also with ease, being able to learn new things from the experience.

Could I have had a melt-down at the very beginning when my truck broke down?

HELL YES!

Would it have helped?

No!

Would I have still solved my problem?

Yes...while also having to purge negative emotions at the same time.

Did I focus on the problem?

Yes...at first.

What did I focus on after I identified the problem?

I focused on possible solutions.

1. Call the dealer to see if they would help me.

2. Sell bigger bundles of my online Psychic/Medium service up front to make more money to pay for the fix.

3. Rent a car and go back home to figure things out.

4. Ask people I trusted for a loan, etc.

Do you see where there is a big difference in focusing on "what could go wrong...negative outputs," and "POSSIBLE SOLUTIONS...positive outputs?"

What were the new core beliefs that I practiced putting into play?

I am abundant. I have more than enough and I am enough.

I am intelligent.

I am trustworthy therefore I can trust.

My Creator Parents, Myself, and the Universe love and support me therefore I am chosen, safe, and loved.

Everything always works out for me.

I am worthy of any and all good things.

If your problem is that you don't have something you want like money, a mate, a house, or a car, etc...then another solution that you should focus on and think about is what you are doing to prepare for having want you want. Yep...make room for it in your life AND your time schedule. For example, there is nothing worse than wanting a mate, and then not making time for them when they do show up in your life...ending up in the end WITHOUT said mate!

Did I feel negative emotions during this time of solving my problem?

YEP...FRUSTRATION!

However, I was able to allow myself to be patient enough to allow the emotion to dissipate before I did anything to move forward in action.

Was I ever without the money I needed?

Surprisingly...NO!

Did I focus on the lack of money?

Awe hell no...I was too busy focusing on possible solutions and having fun with my Son.

Does this easy method work with relationship problems?

Yes.

However, there must be a commitment and willingness to surrender the desired person and outcome, in return for just focusing on ourselves, our well-being, and what we are creating in our own world.

For instance, say you are in love with someone that doesn't reciprocate your feelings. How do you solve a problem like this? Well first you have to look at why the situation exists. This could be for at least 4 reasons or more.

1. They aren't attracted to you.

2. They have soul injuries or fear that keeps them from interacting with you.

3. They are already in a relationship with someone else.

4. You are attracted to them out of a soul injury that they are triggering and you are mistaking the attraction for true love.

What you want to do here is eliminate focusing on anything and everything about this situation that you cannot control. Also practice NOT FOCUSING on what you don't want.

1. You have no control over how the person you desire feels... so stop focusing on that person outside of just appreciating who they are.

2. You don't want someone that doesn't want or chose you...so don't focus on whether this person notices you or not.

3. You don't want someone that ignores you or that doesn't make you a priority...so don't ignore yourself, and be sure to make how you feel and you the priority here.

4. You don't want someone that is in a relationship or choosing to focus on someone else...so don't focus on who this person is interacting with...AT ALL!

5. You don't want someone that doesn't know how to love, accept, or commit to you...so don't focus on getting them to do that with you, just be giving that focus to yourself.

With that said if you want to turn this situation into a **Win-Win** for you then first tell the your Creator Parents and the Universe that you want to be in a loving relationship with your desired person in a time that is best for you both. Feel how good it would be just to hug this person and hold them in your arms as you ask for them. After this set a time frame in which you are willing to hold space for that person in your life, according to how strong you feel the connection is with them. From there **SURRENDER THIS PERSON COMPLETELY AND STOP FOCUSING ON THEM!** If they keep coming to you in dreams and signs...**KEEP SURRENDERING THEM!** After this, if you really want to attract the attention of your desired person to you then below is what you need to focus on.

1. Focus on making sure that you are having the relationship with yourself that you want from the love of your life.

2. Focus on how you feel and what you are doing about how you feel.

3. Focus on changing and updating outdated childhood core beliefs, and healing your own soul injuries.

4. Focus on making everything about your world feel good, feel warm, feel inviting, and exciting.

5. Focus on filling your days with productivity in creating abundance in all areas of your life...in wealth, in lots of good memories, in joyful activities, and in plenty of rest and good food for fuel.

6. Focus on being grateful for everything in your life.

If the person you desire doesn't choose to come into an interaction with you in the time limit that you set, then there are two courses of action that you can take, with one being just as good as the other. Hold space indefinitely for that person while creating the most fulfilling life possible, with close friends and family, and tons of amazing memories and life lessons. Or...surrender that person that you desire to your Creator Parents and the Universe, and ask them to bring you the closest, strongest, most passionate, best fitting, long lasting romantic partner to you in a time that is best for you both...and in return you will not have any expectation of who they are. After this asking with earnest desire, taking time to feel and know that it will be given to you because you are worthy to have someone to love...then again... surrender the desire and get right back into creating your amazing life!

Will the right person come?

You BETCHA!

Will the wrong people still want you?

Most likely...do you really want to waste your time on it?

Did this work for me?

YES!

Will it work for you?

YES!

Why?

Simply because every way you look at it...**YOU WIN!** You either get the person that you desire in a truly functional and compatible relationship, or you heal the soul injury that attracted you to them and THEN you attract the right mate to yourself, OR...you have an amazing full life in which you have chosen to create a wonderful world based on close platonic connectivity.

You see?

There really is no problems, loss, or separation.

There are only solutions, options, learning more, doing more... and...**BEING MORE!**

CHAPTER 20

You Can Never Un-Know A Thing

Believe it or not, once a human learns to do something...they can never "un-know" it. Albeit a person due to ailments like dementia and/or Alzheimers they it can be forgotten by the brains short term memory, what has been learned will forever be in a person's long-term memory and soul. This is why it is so very important to update outdated childhood core beliefs, and put them into practice until they become habit.

One of the biggest fears in humanity today is the fear of making truckloads of money, and then losing it all due to unfortunate happenings. This is where greed and hording comes from. It comes from the fear of "losing it all and landing in the poorhouse." If this is your fear it would be helpful to know that fear is not real. It is you thinking something bad will happen in the future, and when you give that thought focus and feel that fear, at some point you will create it. With this said it would be helpful for you to look how unfounded you fear of not having enough a little closer, and self-talk yourself right out of it.

This is how you reason yourself right out of your fear, and trust me when I say, you will have to do it more than once before it sticks. You have programmed and taught your brain how to attract and manifest money easily. Now that this is hard-wired in your brain permanently it is part of you and you cannot "un-know" it. So...it's ok if you lose all of your money...maybe this is your Creator Parent's keeping you on your path of destiny and it's time to go in a different direction. Maybe it's just that you are learning a life lesson that someone, or a group of people, have come into your life to teach you about. Maybe it's time to let go of old things so that you can create new and better things to have in your life. Maybe you didn't think to give back enough and your soul was just bringing yourself into balance without your conscious mind knowing about it. Regardless, losing money or things is never a bad thing, it's just a way to learn more, do more, and BE MORE!

There was a time before my Son died that I was making 9-10k a month. Shortly before he died my income plummeted, I got behind on my land payments so much that I almost went into foreclosure, and my credit cards were all maxed out. I knew my Son was going to die and the stress of it all had me in a spiral down that I couldn't pull out of it. Things got so bad that when he died I didn't even have the money to pay to have him cremated and my family had to step up for me. I am forever grateful for that to this day.

It was only after 2 years, hiring a business mentor and his team, and a whole lot of doing soul healing and working on changing my mindset, that I was able to come out of it. The interesting thing was that I not only brought my income back up to the 10k mark, I also paid off all of my debt, bringing my credit score to being over 620 for the first time in my life, and I had added a whole new skill-set of internet and digital marketing to my portfolio. Six months after that two year mark my income sky-rocketed up to 20k per month and I haven't looked back!

What did I learn in that dip?

I learned to not fear death...at all...whether it was mine or someone close to me.

Did I forget how to attract and manifest money?

HELL NO!

I learned to make more.

Is is possible for me to have more dips in my life?

Yes.

Am I afraid of them now?

No!

And this my friend is why there is a high likelihood that not only will I not ever have to go down as far as I did at the point I went down to with the death of my Son, there is a better chance now that I will not ever be without larger amounts of money like that again.

Why do I tell you this?

Because most of our problems are money related.

Also...most of our relationship problems are money related...

...and here is the real kicker.

Once you learn problem solving and how to attract and manifest tons of money you FEEL absolutely abundant. It is from this feeling of abundance that we then gain the confidence to create that same feeling of abundance in meaningful relationships, that we then fill our live up with.

Without further a due let's get into the wrap-up of how to get to the **CORE** of your **PROBLEM** and **SOLVE** it.

1. Start by doing "preventative maintenance" in identifying and changing old, negative, childhood core beliefs into updated more positive ones.

2. When you encounter a problem do what you can to breath deeply to get more oxygen to your brain.

3. Ask your Creator Parents (Source, God, Allah, Mohamed, Buddha, etc.) for help, and be sure to look for and/or listen for the answer. *hint...sometimes they come in thought form or signs around you in the form of animals, people, or number sequences.

4. Clear any emotion from your energy field using various methods like, meditation, sleep, taking a walking, exercising, etc.

5. Take time to close your eyes, picture yourself as a child, and practice kind encouraging self-talk, going over your new more positive core beliefs.

6. Gather information in order to form a plethora of solutions.

Try out each solution until you find the one that works the best for you.

7. After trying each solutions be sure to take a break to refresh your energy, and again, clear any negative emotion that may come up, while also restating your new positive core belief. Be sure to also include more kind self-talk with yourself.

8. Once you find a good solution and you have solved your problem, write down what the problem was and how you solved it, just to commit it to memory faster.

9. Rinse and repeat.

As I told you before, you my find yourself faced with problems where your life, or the life of a loved one is in danger and there is not enough time to go through all the steps above. In that case below a shortened version for emergencies.

1. Take a deep breath and ask your Creator Parents (Source, God, Allah, Mohamed, Buddha, etc.) for help, and be sure to look for and/or listen for the answer. *hint...sometimes they come in thought form our signs around you in the form of animals, people, or number sequences.

2. Clear any emotion from your energy field by hyper-focusing on the solutions at hand, NOT the problem.

3. Listening to your intuition and follow your natural instinct.

4. Fight like hell knowing that you live forever and there is never and end to your story...there are only new beginnings, learning more, doing more, and BEING MORE!

5. Rinse and repeat.

It would be helpful to also remember one more thing while learning this easy problem solving solution. Human beings learn by making mistakes. It is by far the most powerful, effective way that we learn simply because we don't like pain or to be uncomfortable, so it sticks in our memories much faster. There is only ONE you, not two, three or four. You are an amazing ORIGINAL...this means there is NO competition! This also means that you will learning in different timing than everyone else and in different ways. It would be helpful if you would be kind with yourself while you are in a learning curve of mastery, knowing how special and precious you are...and drop any shame or guilt around making mistakes at the door, KAPEESH?

Go in peace...and be blessed...just me...Dawn Maree.